10% Better

Also by Dr Rob Yeung

Some of Dr Rob's recent books include:

The Confidence Project: Your Plan for Personal Growth, Happiness and Success

How To Stand Out: Proven Tactics for Getting Noticed

How To Win: The Argument, the Pitch, the Job, the Race

I Is For Influence: The New Science of Persuasion

E Is For Exceptional: The New Science of Success

Personality: How to Unleash Your Hidden Strengths

Answering Tough Interview Questions For Dummies

10% Better

Easy ways to beat stress, think smarter,
get healthy and achieve any goal

Dr Rob Yeung

JOHN
MURRAY
LEARNING

First published in Great Britain in 2020 by John Murray Learning, an imprint of John Murray Press, a division of Hodder and Stoughton Ltd. An Hachette UK company.

Copyright © Dr Rob Yeung 2020

The right of Dr Rob Yeung to be identified as the Author of the Work has been asserted by him in accordance with the Copyright, Designs and Patents Act 1988.

British Library Cataloguing in Publication Data: a catalogue record for this title is available from the British Library.

ISBN 978 1 473 63422 0

Ebook ISBN 978 1 473 63424 4

This book is for information or educational purposes only and is not intended to act as a substitute for medical advice or treatment. Any person with a condition requiring medical attention should consult a qualified medical practitioner or suitable therapist.

Hachette UK policy is to use papers that are natural, renewable and recyclable products and made from wood grown in sustainable forests. The logging and manufacturing processes are expected to conform to the environmental regulations of the country of origin.

Carmelite House

50 Victoria Embankment

London EC4Y 0DZ

www.hodder.co.uk

To my parents and to Steve – thank you for
making me 1,000% better.

Contents

About the author

Rob Yeung, PhD, is a business psychologist and management consultant. Having worked at top-flight consultancy the Boston Consulting Group and now his own firm Talentspace, he is an in-demand advisor showing clients how to use psychological science to improve their personal and organizational effectiveness. In practice, this often means coaching individuals and working with organizations on motivation, leadership, influence and persuasion, sales success, confidence, change, and high achievement.

As a broadcaster and commentator, he appears on major television shows globally, including the BBC, CNN, and CNBC. He has written for newspapers and been quoted in publications including the *Financial Times*, *Daily Telegraph*, *Guardian*, and *Wall Street Journal*. His internationally best-selling books include *How To Stand Out: Proven Tactics For Getting Noticed* (Capstone) and *E is for Exceptional: The New Science of Success* (Pan Books).

www.robyeung.com

www.instagram.com/doctorrobyeung

www.twitter.com/robyeung

www.facebook.com/drrobyeung

Introduction

'Great things are not done by impulse,
but by a series of small things
brought together.'

Vincent van Gogh

If you're reading this Introduction, then I imagine you would like to be better in some way. Perhaps you would like to be happier or you want to take your career to a new level. Maybe you would like to be more confident when meeting new people. You may want to improve your memory – your ability to absorb and retain new information. Or perhaps you want to lose weight and get into better shape.

Here's the thing, though: you probably don't have a huge amount of time to improve yourself. You don't want to spend hours in therapy or journaling or reflecting on your life and how to change it. Like most busy people, you want results – and you want them now!

The good news is that you *can* be better – you can feel happier, be more confident, boost your memory, and lose weight – and quite quickly, too. Psychologists have identified dozens of tricks, tips, and quirks of the mind that can help nearly everyone achieve precisely these sorts of results. And many of these methods really only take minutes – or sometimes only a handful of seconds – to do.

Yes, relatively simple changes in how we think or behave can make a measurable difference to our success, health, relationships, and happiness. And so *10% Better* contains some of my favourite techniques that will quickly help you to be a better, smarter, happier, healthier you.

Focusing on 'you'

I work as a psychologist and coach. So I'll give you an example of a tip that will take no time to put into practice.

Not long ago, a 40-something client of mine called Elizabeth was feeling rather nervous. She had been widowed several years previously when her husband died of cancer. And now she was preparing to go on a date with a man for the first time in nearly 20 years.

It was perfectly understandable that she was more than a little apprehensive. So I suggested that she could buoy her mood and feel a bit more confident by repeating encouraging messages to herself.

'I already do that,' she told me. 'I often say things to myself like, "I can do this," "I'm stronger than I feel," and "I can achieve anything I put my mind to."'

I suggested: 'Ah, you would get better results if you talked to yourself as if you're a separate person.'

'What do you mean?' she asked.

'You could rephrase those encouraging statements either by using the word "you" or by using your own name,' I explained. 'So rather than saying, "I can do this," say, "You can do this" or "Elizabeth can do this."'

Like most of the advice that I give to clients, this little trick has been proven in scientific tests to have genuine benefits. Some years ago, a team of scientists led by Ethan Kross, a professor of psychology at the University of Michigan, trained multiple groups of people in the use of different types of self-talk prior to stressful situations. In their experiment, 89 participants were told that they would soon be giving an impromptu speech to a group of total strangers.

I don't know about you, but I know plenty of people who hate having to stand up and give speeches in public. So you can imagine that a lot of these participants felt fairly stressed by the prospect of having to give such a speech.

Half of the participants were told to prepare mentally by using the first-person pronoun 'I' when thinking about themselves. The other half of the participants were taught to use either the pronoun 'you' or their own names.

Cutting a long story short, the participants who used the pronoun 'you' or their own names performed significantly better than those who used the first-person pronoun 'I'. The participants who used 'you' or their names reported feeling less stressed than those who used 'I'. In addition, the 'you'/names participants were also judged by observers to have given visibly better presentations. In other words, the 'you'/names participants not only subjectively felt better – they objectively performed better, too.

If you're interested in the specifics of this study – or any of the others that we encounter – you can read more by following the superscript numbers to the Notes at the end of the book.[1] But the broader implication of Kross's experiment is: the next time you need to motivate yourself, try encouraging yourself as if you were talking to someone else.

When you want to push yourself on at the gym, spur yourself on before a big job interview or date (like Elizabeth), or encourage yourself to get through a difficult task, tell yourself: 'You can do it!' rather than 'I can do it!' And remember that the research says that you may not just feel better but perform better, too.

> The next time you need to motivate yourself, try encouraging yourself as if you were talking to someone else.

Using psychological techniques that work

Before we get into deeper discussion about other such tweaks and advice, allow me to introduce myself briefly. I work as a psychologist, consultant, and coach. In practice, that means I run training workshops for teams of executives and employees. I give keynote speeches to audiences full of managers, charity workers, sales people, personal trainers, students – all sorts of people. And I coach individuals one-on-one. But in all of my work, I have to be a professional sceptic.

It's my job to question what comes my way and only recommend techniques that really work. I can't just believe all of the claims that I come across. And I don't think it would be fair merely to tell you in this book what to do without justifying my recommendations to you either.

I think it's especially important these days to be somewhat sceptical and questioning. Everywhere we look – television, billboards, Facebook, emails – we get bombarded about products that can allegedly change our lives in all sorts of wonderful ways. There are supposed superfoods and supplements that are touted as being able to burn fat, reverse diabetes, or even treat cancer. Gadgets that can help to boost our productivity or cure hair loss. Online courses that can make us charismatic, lovable, or rich.

> It's especially important these days to be somewhat sceptical and questioning.

Some of these products may have merit. But many don't. And unfortunately there are plenty of frauds, quacks, scammers, or even well-intentioned but poorly informed gurus who simply can't deliver on their promises.

When I hear about new products and services, treatments, and therapies, I usually think: 'Really? What's the evidence for that?' It's my job to protect clients from harm by proposing only things that work. And in the same way, I feel it's my job to keep you safe.

But I don't just want to tell you about methods that work – I would also love by the end of this book for you to have adopted a similarly questioning attitude in life. So when *you* next encounter any new product, therapy or piece of advice, I hope that you too will stop and ask: 'Really? What's the evidence for that?'

It's not just about proof, though. I also want my clients to find it easy or even enjoyable to integrate new methods and techniques into their lives. There's no point having me suggest something that clients think would be too complicated or bothersome to try even once – let alone do over and over again. And so I'll only include things in this book if I think they are effective and easy – and occasionally even enjoyable.

In chapter after chapter, we'll discuss how you can perform more effectively under pressure, how you can get fitter and lose more weight, and how you can live a happier life. We'll discuss how you can come across more confidently in job interviews, during auditions, and on dates. We'll explore the latest science about learning and memory, creativity, and being in a happy relationship. And we'll even see that there can be genuine merit in asking: 'What would Batman do?'

Becoming 10% better

Yes, you will learn to deal with stress, get fitter and lose weight, be more creative, and so on. But I think it's important to have realistic expectations.

I called this book *10% Better* because I think it's completely achievable that you can improve yourself in these sorts of areas by double digits. Take the study by Ethan Kross and his colleagues that we discussed earlier. The researchers found that participants who referred to themselves using either the word 'you' or their own names felt around 20% better than participants who used the first-person pronoun 'I'. And when expert observers watched the presentations and scored everyone's performances, they gave the 'you'/names participants ratings that were approximately 10% better.

In terms of eating, I'll share with you one tip that has been shown to reduce unhealthy snacking on things like cookies by 24%. And another suggestion may help you to cut down on your calorie intake by as much as 36%.

The list goes on. For example, I will tell you about a particular method for setting goals that in one study allowed students to get 13% better results in a written exam.

Every single technique, method, tweak, tip, and piece of advice in this book has been tested by science. Some deliver bigger benefits. Others deliver smaller – but still meaningful – results. Add up all of these and you may well end up being quite a bit more than 10% better.

Navigating this book

I've divided the book into eight chapters and a conclusion. But *10% Better* isn't a book where you need to read each chapter in order to understand the one that follows. So feel free to jump around. For example, if you most want to get fit or lose weight, then head straight to Chapter 3. Or if you're studying for a test or exam, you may find Chapter 6 a more useful starting point.

Honestly, each chapter stands alone. So do skip forwards and backwards between chapters if that sounds most helpful. In order to decide where to head first, here's a quick summary of each of the coming chapters:

- **Chapter 1: Getting smart about stress and everyday pressures.** Maybe your computer deleted all of your work, you've just had an argument, or you just feel overwhelmed by everything you have to do. There are very few people who don't feel stressed, anxious, worried, or angry at least occasionally. In this first chapter, we'll look at speedy methods that you can use to get through tough times.

- **Chapter 2: Boosting your motivation and achieving your goals.** We all have goals but it isn't always easy to reach them. Perhaps you want a better job or a more fulfilling romantic life. Maybe you want to change some aspect of your personality or modify your behaviour – quit a bad habit or start a good one, for instance. Staying motivated can be tricky, but in this chapter we will look at some research-backed advice to improve your chances of achieving your goals.

- **Chapter 3: Being smart about health and weight loss.** As you can imagine, a lot of people have goals that are to do with their physical health and weight loss in particular. Chapter 2 will cover tweaks that can be applied to all sorts of goals. But in this chapter, you will learn a set of techniques that will help you to achieve your health, eating, and weight loss goals.

- **Chapter 4: Making better decisions.** Maybe you're trying to decide on a new phone or a laptop, a car or a pension plan. Or perhaps you're trying to decide whether to take a new job, relocate to a new city, or end your relationship. Sometimes, the wrong choice could cost you money; occasionally, the wrong decision could leave you with regrets for years or even decades to come. Thankfully, psychological science has identified a handful of methods that will allow you to make all sorts of decisions with greater confidence.

- **Chapter 5: Boosting your creativity and inventiveness.** Creativity isn't just something for artists – it's a vital skill for anyone who wants to find new, better, faster, cheaper, more enjoyable ways of doing things. It's as relevant to someone who wants to get the household chores done more quickly and less painfully as to an entrepreneur who wants to offer something more interesting to customers. And in this chapter we'll see that spending just a few minutes on various mental activities and exercises can make a marked difference to people's ability to think, work, and be better.

- **Chapter 6: Being clever about learning, memory, and performance.** Learning isn't just something that was confined to our school days. *Life* is a constant process of learning. At work, you constantly need to learn the latest rules and new ways of working. You have to adapt to new operating systems on computers and new smartphones. You may need to take an exam to attain a professional qualification. Perhaps you want to learn a new language, sport, or musical instrument. Or you want to improve your assertiveness, financial acumen, emotional intelligence, leadership skills, or anything else about yourself. It's all learning. So in this chapter, you'll learn how to learn better.

- **Chapter 7: Dealing with pressure and performing in public.** This chapter will be of particular use in high-stakes situations when you're being judged by people in a public setting. So maybe you want to give a great presentation, speak up more at work, succeed at job interviews, or make a good impression on a hot date. Or perhaps you're an athlete, singer, musician, or other performer who needs to perform under pressure.

- **Chapter 8: Finding small ways to feel happier.** Life is not always easy. But research tells us that straightforward exercises can help us to find more moments of joy and contentment in our everyday lives – or extend and heighten the moments that come our way. So turn to this chapter if you'd like to feel happier.

- **Conclusions: Onwards, upwards, and over to you.** By the time we get to the end of the book, we will have covered dozens and dozens of exercises, methods, and activities. So I'll finish by leaving you with some advice on how to get the most from them all.

Over to you

I write books because I hope that I can help people to have better, more productive, effective, successful, and happier lives. So throughout *10% Better*, I'll try to make it easy for you to pick out and apply the many techniques that we shall encounter. Look out for boxes just like this one for step-by-step guidance on how to put the different principles or techniques into practice to benefit either your professional or personal life.

1

Getting smart about stress and everyday pressures

'We are not creatures of circumstance;
we are creators of circumstance.'

Benjamin Disraeli

One of my clients, a manager I'll call Brendan, often spends 10 or 12 hours a day at his stressful job – yet never gets offered the promotion he craves. He'd love to get a new job, but he doesn't feel that he has the time or energy to investigate better opportunities.

Another client called Anya has just separated from her husband and is working through the legalities of getting divorced. Their two teenage children have been quite distressed by the split: one has become surly and uncommunicative, while the other has become argumentative and aggressive. Anya feels that the stress within her personal life is wrecking her concentration and performance at work.

Peter works as a graphic designer for a large law firm. But shortly after his 40th birthday, he decided that he wanted to change careers. He is now trying to set up his own business working as an interior designer on evenings and weekends. In addition, he and his wife want to start a family and have been through several rounds of in vitro fertilization (IVF) treatment, which have been expensive, time-consuming, and stressful.

Stress seems to be pretty much a central part of modern-day life. The cause of stress doesn't have to be one thing – it can result from the build-up of work difficulties, family conflicts, money troubles, relationship issues, injuries and illnesses, and day-to-day worries and hassles.

> The cause of stress doesn't have to be one thing – it can result from the build-up of work difficulties, family conflicts, money troubles, relationship issues, injuries and illnesses, and day-to-day worries and hassles.

How often do you feel that you have too many things to do? How often do you feel irritable or frustrated, tense, or discouraged? How often would you say that you're doing things because you have to rather than because you want to?

These are the sorts of questions that researchers have typically asked when measuring people's stress levels. For example, researchers led by Sheldon Cohen at Carnegie-Mellon University devised the Perceived Stress Scale back in 1983. It's one of the most frequently used measures of stress in the world – and has been used in thousands and thousands of studies all over the world.[1]

Another popular test, called the Perceived Stress Questionnaire, was created a decade later by a team of psychologists led by Susan Levenstein of Nuovo Regina Margherita Hospital in Italy. This investigative team added hugely to the field of stress research by establishing that high levels of perceived stress could trigger physical illnesses, such as ulcerative colitis.[2] So stress isn't just something that affects us psychologically – it can have debilitating effects on our bodies and physical health, too.

But what both of these tests have in common is that they measure *perceived* stress. So stress isn't about what is going on in the world around you. It's about how you think and feel and see the world and yourself. If you *feel* tired or frustrated, lonely or isolated, then that is stress. It doesn't matter what your actual situation may be. Simply *thinking* that you are under pressure from other people or loaded down with responsibility is enough to trigger the psychological and physiological changes that make up the stress response.

You have no doubt heard advice about getting massages, doing physical exercise, taking soothing baths, or performing meditation in order to beat stress. But I'm going to introduce you to some advice that you probably won't have come across before.

As I said, stress occurs when you think or feel a certain way; with only a little effort you can make a deliberate choice to feel better. So we're going to look at a handful of ways of tackling stress by changing how you think or focusing your attention in unusual ways.

> Stress isn't about what is going on in the world around you. It's about how you think and feel and see the world and yourself.

Ecphorizing happy memories

I had a notification on my smartphone a few days ago. Bear with me and I'll explain how it relates to coping with stress.

Exactly three years ago, our family dog chewed a box of tissues. He's a gentle, sweet-natured dog, a fluffy and playful Miniature Schnauzer. But he does like to chew tissues. And for some reason on that day, I left a stack of tissues on a low stool before leaving him alone at home.

When I returned a few hours later, there were shredded pieces of tissue everywhere. Dozens and dozens of scraps, fragments, and tatters of white tissue paper. And our dog, Byron, was just sitting amongst it all, as if he had had nothing to do with it.

It was a comical scene. After all, he had chewed tissues in the past so it was my own silly fault for having left the tissues within easy reach. It would be a minor bother to clean up. I laughed and grabbed my phone to take pictures of the carnage.

Anyway, today my Google Photos app sent me a notification, inviting me to 'rediscover this day'. So I did. And it made me smile.

Google Photos sends me a handful of reminders every week. Facebook sends me similar reminders, too. Last week it told me: 'Rob, we care about you and the memories that you share here. We thought that you'd like to look back on this post from 2 years ago.'

Have you ever reminisced fondly over old pictures – perhaps on social media or even a physical photograph in an album or one you have had framed? If the answer is 'yes', then you have engaged in something called ecphory. Hans Markowitsch, a professor and researcher in the psychology of memory at the University of Bielefeld in Germany, defines ecphory as 'the process by which retrieval cues interact with stored information so that an image or a representation of the information in question appears.'[3]

That's a rather technical, psychological definition. But to me, ecphory simply means using a cue in the real world to trigger information stored in the brain to recall a memory.

So yes, you could ecphorize by looking at either images on a screen or actual photographs in your hand. You could ecphorize by picking up a memento or keepsake that sets off a particular memory – perhaps a pebble that reminds you of a beach holiday or a smell that takes you back to a childhood birthday. You could even ecphorize by reading a particular phrase such as, 'One of your happiest moments in the last few years' or 'A positive memory about a good friend.'

> Ecphory simply means using a cue in the real world to trigger information stored in the brain to bring about a memory.

This chapter is about techniques that can be used to beat stress. So of course I'm arguing that ecphory – the simple act of reminiscing about happy moments from the past – can help in the battle against stress. But is there any serious evidence that it works?

Rutgers University research psychologists Megan Speer and Mauricio Delgado decided to investigate this precise issue. In a recent study, they deliberately subjected a group of experimental participants to a stress-inducing situation – and then tested whether a few minutes of recalling positive memories would make a difference to participants' stress levels.

The participants underwent something called the socially evaluative cold pressor test. The cold pressor test involves asking participants to plunge their hands and wrists into a vat of freezing cold water for as long as possible.

Honestly, that's pretty uncomfortable. Try it yourself if you dare. Within seconds, you'll probably find yourself gritting your teeth and screwing up your face against the numbing pain in your hands.

But the participants in this study were put through an even tougher, so-called socially evaluative version of the test. They were additionally told that they would be videotaped so that their facial expressions could later be analysed by experts; they were instructed to look directly into a camera lens. Most people don't even like to have their voices captured in recordings – so imagine how justifiably awkward they felt having their agonized facial expressions caught on camera.

All of the participants were subjected to the cold pressor test and were filmed. Immediately afterwards, they were split into two groups. One (the experimental) group was asked to spend a few minutes recalling positive memories. The other (the control) group was asked to spend the same amount of time recalling neutral memories. (I'm sure you've heard of the placebo effect: the fact that people can sometimes feel better even when they have done a sham exercise or bogus treatment. So by including a control group, the researchers were able to test whether recalling positive memories was genuinely more effective at reducing stress than a placebo activity.)

Finally, all of the participants completed questionnaires about their stress levels. They also provided saliva samples so the researchers could monitor their levels of cortisol, the stress hormone. Oh, and remember that all of the participants had been asked to recall either positive or neutral memories *after* the stress-inducing test.

As you might expect, the researchers did indeed find a benefit from recalling positive memories. Participants who recalled positive memories after the freezing cold water test reported feeling significantly better than participants who recalled neutral memories. In addition, participants who recalled positive moments had far smaller increases in cortisol than the control participants.[4] In other words, ecphorizing – being prompted to recall positive memories – may reduce both psychological and physiological levels of stress.

> Ecphorizing – being prompted to recall positive memories – may reduce both psychological and physiological levels of stress.

This is a great experiment for a couple of reasons. First of all, the researchers measured both mental and bodily indicators of stress. So ecphory did not just change people's subjective, emotional reaction to stress, which critics may argue are ephemeral and therefore don't really matter. The technique also dampened down the body's objective, hormonal reaction to stress, which suggests that it could have medical benefits, too.

The inclusion of a control group is also important. Being prompted to recall neutral memories was not enough to dampen the stress response. No, the act of mere recollection was not enough. It was only when participants were told to cast their minds back to *positive* memories that led to a reduced response to stress.

The enterprising researchers Speer and Delgado concluded: 'When uncontrolled, psychological stress can drive us far from a desirable state, enhancing positive feelings by reminiscing about the past may be one way to bring us back.' Or, to use plain English: if you're feeling bad, simply making an effort to remember happier times may help you to feel better.

Cueing your own happy memories

Life often throws unexpected challenges at us. And ecphory – using real-world cues to trigger happy memories – may be a handy technique to have in our armoury of stress-busting techniques.

Remember that ecphory involves using external cues. Typically, researchers have used words or phrases, because these tend to be meaningful to everyone. But you could potentially try using more personal cues, such as photos, physical objects, mementoes, sounds, or songs. If you wish to cue your own positive memories using phrases alone, you could use the following, which are based on prompts used by Hans Markowitsch's team:

- The first positive memory in your life that you can truly remember.
- A positive event from your childhood, e.g. a play situation.
- A happy childhood birthday.
- A positive memory involving a good friend.
- A pleasant holiday you once had.
- A time you felt in love.

- A happy, cheerful, or amusing adventure you once had.
- A delightful situation you shared with someone.
- A time you experienced success.
- The happiest moment you have had in the last few years.
- A moment you felt motivated and positive.
- A joyful situation.
- A time you enjoyed a pleasant, intimate experience.
- An occasion you felt very enthusiastic.

The beauty of this technique is that you can recall whatever memories *you* find pleasant. Just focus on a handful of happy memories for several minutes. And that really is all you need to do.

At this point, perhaps you're still not entirely convinced about this ecphory technique. It just sounds far too easy. And, to be honest, if some random person had told me that simply spending a couple of minutes reminiscing about happier times could beat stress I would have raised a very quizzical eyebrow. But allow me to provide you with even more compelling evidence that it works.

Neuroscientists often use functional magnetic resonance imaging (fMRI) equipment to peer into the workings of the brain. And researchers have found that the deceptively simple act of re-experiencing pleasant memories actually has effects on the brain that are eminently detectable. Megan Speer and a new team of collaborators found that recalling positive autobiographical memories led to increased activity in the striatum, ventral medial prefrontal cortex, orbitofrontal cortex, and anterior cingulate.

Now, these regions of the brain are of particular interest as they are generally involved in processing the effects of rewards, such as money. In theory, this pattern of brain activation should mean that merely savouring happier times should be as rewarding to the brain as receiving a cash prize.

So Speer and her colleagues set about testing this hypothesis. They created an elaborate game in which participants could choose to recall either a positive memory or a neutral memory (e.g. a recent trip to go grocery shopping) in return for small cash prizes. The cash prizes changed every time: sometimes more cash was offered for one or other type of memory. And sometimes the cash rewards for the two were the same.

When the cash prizes for recalling either the positive memory or the neutral memory were the same, participants chose to recall positive memories 85% of the time. That's not too surprising a result.

But when more cash was offered for recalling the neutral memory, participants still sometimes chose to savour the positive memory. In fact, participants were willing to give up 28% of their potential earnings to recall positive rather than neutral memories. In other words, reminiscing about happier times was sometimes really worth more to participants than actual cash that they could take away and spend.[5]

To me, then, there's extremely compelling evidence for the power of ecphory, the seemingly humble act of using cues to remind ourselves of happier times. We know that recalling happy memories reduces both psychological and physiological markers of stress. It also stimulates the reward centres of the brain. *And* it's such an intense motivator that laboratory participants sometimes forgo real cash prizes simply for the right to savour positive moments. Not bad for a tweak that costs nothing and can take mere moments to do.

There's extremely compelling evidence for the power of ecphory, the seemingly humble act of using cues to remind ourselves of happier times.

Learning to soldier on in the face of stress

Can you imagine how stressed you might feel to have people shooting at you and trying to kill you? Imagine having to wonder whether your next step might be on an explosive device that could blow off both of your legs. Or how you might feel to see friends losing their limbs or dying in front of you.

Those are just a few of the immediate stressors – sources of stress – facing people in the armed forces. But they also have to cope with ongoing stressors, too: being perhaps thousands of miles away from their families for months at a time, living on rations, being cooped up in military compounds, and feeling bored when they're off duty.

Due to the stress that military personnel must endure, researchers have been scurrying to figure out what helps them to stay both physically and psychologically healthy. And it turns out that a key factor is their outlook on life.

To measure the extent to which you feel in control of and see meaning in your life, take a look at just six statements derived from a psychological questionnaire created by Sigurd Hystad, a psychosocial scientist at the University of Bergen in Norway.[6] I'll present the statements to you in two sets of three.

To what extent would you agree with these three statements?

- 'I spend most of my life doing things that are meaningful.'
- 'It is up to me to decide how the rest of my life will turn out.'
- 'Most of the time, life is interesting and exciting for me.'

Then consider another three statements. Again, to what extent would you say you agree or disagree with these?

- 'I think there is not much I can do to influence my own future.'
- 'I feel that my life is fairly empty of meaning.'
- 'I feel that life in general is boring for me.'

When Hystad and his colleagues asked 7,239 military men and women to complete questionnaires containing similar statements, they were able to detect certain patterns of health and sickness. There was a clear relationship between the extent to which personnel felt out of control and the number of medically certified sickness absences they took.

The more that personnel agreed with the first three statements, the more they tended to be protected against sickness. But the more that they agreed with the second three statements, the more likely they were to fall ill over the subsequent twelve-month period.[7]

So take a look back at those six statements. Do you feel that you spend enough of your time doing things that are meaningful? To what extent do you feel that you can influence your own future? Are you making decisions and feeling in charge of your life or merely drifting and feeling bored?

> Do you feel that you spend enough of your time doing things that are meaningful?

These seem like massive questions about life. But two subsequent research studies have shown that you can change your outlook on life quite quickly.

In one study, German researchers led by Tobias Teismann at Ruhr University Bochum asked 64 adult men and women

to write about one of two topics. Participants in an experimental group were asked to project themselves forwards in
time and to write about how they imagined their lives might
turn out.

But the researchers were smart enough to realize that simply
the act of writing in itself – about almost any topic – might
have some kind of minor benefit, like that of a placebo. So
they asked a second (control) group of participants to spend
the same length of time writing about mundane topics, such
as their journeys to work or how they typically went about
cleaning their kitchens.

After the writing exercises, the researchers noticed that those
who had written about their future lives reported a modest
decrease in worrisome thinking compared to the control participants. But here's the clever bit. Rather than just looking
at intangible, ephemeral thoughts and feelings, the researchers
also decided to measure the participants' biological responses
to stress. So all of the participants provided multiple saliva samples, allowing the researchers to check for the presence of the
stress hormone cortisol.

As you might expect, participants in the experimental group
who wrote about their life goals benefitted more. They exhib-
ited lower levels of cortisol than the control participants who
wrote about routine, everyday activities. And the difference was
measurable for a full 48 hours after the writing exercises.[8]

In other words, writing about life goals did not just calm
unruly thoughts. It also had a quantifiable benefit in terms of
the participants' physiologies that lasted two days.

But a second study suggests that the benefits of writing about
life goals may last even longer. Across the Atlantic Ocean and
over 4,800 miles away, a separate squad of scientists led by Steve

Harrist, a researcher at Oklahoma State University, asked several dozen university student participants to spend 20 minutes writing about their life goals. The participants were given the instructions:

Think about your life in the future. Imagine that everything has gone as well as it possibly could. You have worked hard and succeeded at accomplishing all of your life goals. Think of this as the realization of all of your life dreams. Now, write about what you have imagined.

As with the other researchers, Harrist and his colleagues were watchful that the simple act of writing in itself might have some kind of minor, placebo benefit. So they also asked a second group of participants to spend the same amount of time writing about their schedules, the tasks they needed to do in life.

The researchers then kept track of the number of times that participants visited the university's health centre because of illness. And, over the course of the next three months, students who had written about their future lives visited the health centre significantly fewer times for illness than students who had written about their schedule.

Clearly, writing about life goals can have important benefits for your health. But do you really have to write about your life goals? Could you talk about them instead?

Writing about life goals can have important benefits for your health.

Thankfully, Harrist's team wondered the same thing. So they included two further groups of participants. A third group was given almost the same written 'Think about your life in the future' instructions as the first. But rather than writing about their life goals, these participants spent 20 minutes speaking out loud about them to another person. And a fourth group spent the same amount of time talking about a neutral topic to another person. Again, the researchers tracked the number of illness-related visits that these further participants made to the health centre.

When the researchers scrutinized the data from all four groups, they found that both writing and talking about life goals were equally protective. Whether participants wrote about their life goals or spoke about them to another person, they had better health over the next three months than others who either wrote or spoke about a less important topic.[9]

There was one notable difference between the writing and talking groups, though. Participants in the talking group rated the task as having been more difficult than those who had written about it. Participants found it easier to write about their life goals than to speak about them. And to me, that makes sense. For example, if I ask you to multiply 19 by 87 using pencil and paper to work out the answer, it's a relatively straightforward exercise. However, if I insist that you do the same multiplication only by talking through the steps out loud, that's a lot harder. You would probably find that it took pretty much all of your mental resources – and you still might not get to the right answer.

It's so much easier to structure our thoughts when we write rather than simply talk out loud. And so for that reason, I usually recommend to my clients that they write – or type – their life goals as opposed to discussing them or merely thinking about them privately.

> It's so much easier to structure our thoughts when
> we write rather than simply talk out loud.

As with the ecphory exercise that we encountered at the start of the chapter, it's almost difficult to believe that a humble little writing exercise could protect our physical health for at least three months. But it does.

Envisioning the future to boost your health

There's very solid research showing that stress increases people's likelihood of experiencing ill health. For example, a British study following 7,268 men and women over an 18-year period found that people who said that stress affected their health 'a lot or extremely' were more than twice as likely to die of heart disease than those who reported no effects of stress on their health.[10] Clearly, stress can be a really big deal.

But studies by multiple groups of researchers have found that a simple exercise can have measurable benefits for people's physical health. Granted, it's not a superfast tweak that can be done in only a few minutes. But wouldn't 20 minutes of your time – that's still a tiny fraction of a day – be worth it for a significant boost to your health?

To give this exercise a go, you could work through the following instructions, which are based on guidelines used by Tobias Teismann and his colleagues.

Imagine it's your 75th birthday and you've thrown a party for all of the important people in your life. Everything in your life has gone well and you've achieved all of the goals that you set for yourself. Now imagine that your guests are giving speeches about you and the life you have lived. What would your party guests have to say about you?

Remember that Steve Harrist's participants reported that they found it easier to do this kind of exercise in writing. However, his study also found that you should still be able to get the protective effect by talking about your future life – although you'll of course need to find a friend who is willing to listen to you for the same length of time.

Why does writing about future goals reduce stress? When I recommend this exercise to clients, they often tell me that it reminds them what's important and therefore what's less important. The exercise helps them to do away with less critical activities that might have been distracting them from what really matters. Other clients say that it helps them to keep things in perspective – to strengthen their resolve and keep them motivated.

Almost everybody is so busy these days that it's easy to get caught up doing things, catching up with work and simply running, running, running to keep on top of all of the tasks we feel we should be doing. But it seems that focusing on what matters and is meaningful to us may help to inoculate us against stress and even protect our physical health. So consider that this writing exercise is the kind of important activity that may be worth planning into your schedule.

> Focusing on what matters and is meaningful to us may help to inoculate us from stress and even protect our physical health.

Feeling on top of technology

Sometimes science points to solutions that can seem fairly mundane. As an example, allow me to present you with four possible solutions for reducing stress at work. One of these has been shown to be a proven method for helping people to feel less stressed. Can you guess which one it is?

So here are your contenders:

- Switching off your smartphone for just 20 minutes during every workday.
- Checking your email fewer times during the course of the day.
- Removing all clocks and watches from the vicinity of your desk.
- Culling the number of friends you have on Facebook by 20%.

So which of the four actions do you think has been demonstrated by scientists to reduce the stress that people experience at work? Go on, place your bet.

After all, there has been a lot of discussion – not just in the popular press but also amongst serious academics – about the issue of people becoming ever-more dependent or even addicted to their smartphones. A lot of workers also complain about the sheer volume of emails they receive. Yes, email is a method for almost instantaneously sending information pretty much anywhere in the world – but you don't often hear people talking about how much they are looking forward to wading through their email inboxes.

Removing all clocks and watches is just something I thought of off the top of my head. And while culling your Facebook friends may or may not be beneficial, I don't actually know of any studies that have proven it to have a de-stressing effect.

It's actually checking email less often that reduces stress. Again, this was tested in an experimental study. In this case, University of British Columbia psychological scientists Kostadin Kushlev and Elizabeth Dunn obtained permission to track the daily stress and well-being levels of 124 employees over a two-week period.

During one week, the participants were encouraged to check their emails as many times as they liked. For the second week, they were instructed to check their email only three times a day – and to keep their mailbox closed and to turn off all new email alerts the rest of the time.

On analysing the results, the researchers discovered that checking email fewer times a day was associated with a wide range of benefits. On those days, participants reported feeling significantly less stressed – in particular they felt less tense. But they also said that they felt more productive and more socially connected to the people around them; they even reported sleeping noticeably better at night.

Granted, none of these changes was massive. However, they were all large enough to be measurable. And all by simply checking emails fewer times a day and turning off all email functions the rest of the time.

The researchers also asked the participants to report how many times they did actually check their emails every day. On average, people said that they checked their email around 13 times a day when given unlimited permission and around five times a day when they had in fact been told to check email only three times a day. But even though most participants had failed to stick to the more restrictive three times a day, they still reported benefits in terms of lower stress, enhanced productivity, feelings of social connectedness, and better sleep.[11]

So could you check your email just five times a day? Perhaps when you first get into the office, then at 11 a.m., lunchtime, 3 p.m., and for a final time as you are finishing up at work?

Of course, I follow this advice myself. Whenever I first sit down at my computer, I check my email. But then I close down my email before I start anything else – creating the slides for a client workshop or writing a chapter of a book, for example. Having no notifications means that I can concentrate fully on whatever I want to be doing. Then I'll wait until I've finished a decent chunk of work before allowing myself to check my emails again.

Why does checking email less frequently reduce stress? It may be largely to do with what are called switching costs. Psychologists know that there is typically a cognitive cost whenever we swap one task for another.

Suppose for a moment that you're writing a report and receive a ping telling you that a new email has landed in your inbox. But dealing with the email may interrupt your thought processes about the report. Maybe you had a good idea but then forgot it. Or it just takes you a few seconds to immerse yourself in the purpose and content of the report again.

Anyway, those lost moments represent a switching cost. There have been dozens of studies looking at switching costs from all manner of different tasks and the strong conclusion is that people are usually slower or less accurate – or both – whenever they have to transition from one task to another.

Many of the people I work with complain about the volume of emails they face daily – most get dozens and dozens, while some even get a couple of hundred a day. Add up all of those daily email interruptions and that could amount to a real hit to your performance, productivity, and stress levels.

> Add up all of those daily email interruptions and that could amount to a real hit to your performance, productivity, and stress levels.

Now, you may be thinking that you couldn't possibly check your email fewer times a day. But remember that the study found that the 124 workers who tried it overall reported multiple benefits in terms of reduced stress and even better sleep. So what have you got to lose by giving it a go?

Reframing the experience of stress and strong emotions

Have you ever felt not just a little stressed but fairly distressed or even overwhelmed at work? It hasn't happened to me for many years, but I once closed my office door, sat on the floor with my back to the door, and cried.

This was early in my career when I was in my mid-20s. I was working at a small consulting firm and for quite a while had been feeling unsupported and even undermined by the company's chairman.

But it was a specific incident that set me off. The *Financial Times* – probably the UK's most prestigious business publication – had agreed to publish an article of mine on the psychology of leaders and their teams. It was a major achievement as not one of my colleagues had ever managed it. But when I told the chairman about it, he ordered that I should take my name off the article and put a colleague's name on it instead.

I had put in the hours pitching ideas to the newspaper's editor then researching the article and writing it. But the chairman insisted that one of his favourite employees – who didn't even *know* about the article let alone contribute to it – should have her name on the byline.

I had already been feeling rather low. But this felt so incredibly unfair. And I couldn't help myself from crying at work, although only my office mate – a good friend – saw me doing it.

Often, conveying distress and sharing it with others – for example by talking about it, complaining to colleagues, or even crying – can be a way of feeling better. Researchers Eileen Kennedy-Moore and Jeanne Watson once concluded in a review of the evidence in this field that 'In daily life, people seek out opportunities to talk about their feelings' and that emotional 'expression can be a means of alleviating distress'.[12]

> If you have ever grumbled to a colleague or had a proper cry, you will know how cathartic it can be to express your distress.

But you may know this for yourself. If you have ever grumbled to a colleague or had a proper cry, you will know how cathartic it can be to express your distress – to allow yourself to appear sad or anxious or frustrated rather than having to pretend you're fine.

Unfortunately, doing what feels good may not always be good for your career. Rightly or wrongly, a lot of managers think that there's no place for emotion at work – certainly not negative emotions, in any case. They may feel embarrassed or uncomfortable about seeing visible displays of anguish in others. After all, emotion is often seen as the opposite of rational thinking. And surely work is all about doing the rational, logical thing, isn't it?

So we have a problem. On the one hand, psychological research suggests that talking about problems, having a grumble, and even crying may help us to feel better. On the other hand, the informal rules of work tell us that we should keep negative feelings and emotional displays to ourselves.

> The informal rules of work tell us that we should keep negative feelings and emotional displays to ourselves.

A quartet of researchers led by Harvard Business School's Elizabeth Baily Wolf wondered if there might be a solution to the problem. Consider the following paragraph, which the researchers showed to just over 50 American employees:

> Samuel works in the advertising department of a large firm. He is currently working with three co-workers on a team. Samuel has become increasingly sad with the team dynamic. One day he breaks down and begins crying in front of his teammates. He buries his face in his hands and says, 'I'm sorry. I am just really emotional about this.'

A second group – again of just over 50 employees – reads an almost identical paragraph:

> Samuel works in the advertising department of a large firm. He is currently working with three co-workers on a team. Samuel has become increasingly sad with the team dynamic. One day he breaks down and begins crying in front of his teammates. He buries his face in his hands and says, 'I'm sorry. I am just really passionate about this.'

A third group reads yet another, again slightly different, paragraph:

> Samuel works in the advertising department of a large firm. He is currently working with three

co-workers on a team. Samuel has become increasingly sad with the team dynamic. One day he breaks down and begins crying in front of his teammates. He buries his face in his hands and says, 'I'm sorry.'

Can you spot the differences between the three? In the first instance, we see that Samuel says that he feels 'emotional'. In the second paragraph, he describes himself as 'passionate'. And for the third group, he apologizes, but gives no reason for his emotional display.

It doesn't seem like a big difference – more word play than anything meaningful. Yet this small change of wording did have measurable effects. Participants who read about Samuel feeling 'passionate' rated him significantly more positively than when he said that he was either 'emotional' or when he gave no further explanation. They said that Samuel seemed more powerful and that he should be more worthy of a leadership position. They also said that he came across as more competent, capable, confident, and even intelligent.

When the researchers ran further studies with real people telling stories of when they had been emotional at work, they found a similar result. People who attribute their emotional distress to passion get rated more highly than people who merely blame their emotions.

> People who attribute their emotional distress to passion get rated more highly than people who merely blame their emotions.

However, the researchers weren't done. They had another set of questions: is displaying negative emotion at work a good thing at all? Or should we all try to hide our emotions full stop? So they ran a final experiment.

This time, the researchers created three stories about a fictitious individual who said that he felt 'upset'. In one version, the individual said that he was so upset because he 'felt so passionate about' a situation at work. In a second version, the individual said nothing extra. And in the third version, the individual said that he felt upset but successfully 'hid how I was feeling in front of my co-workers'.

As before, the individual who felt 'passionate' was rated more highly than the individual who said nothing about why he was upset. However, this time it was the person who hid his feelings who was rated the most highly.[13]

In other words, yes, attributing a display or outburst of negative emotion to passion can make things better than not saying anything at all. However, the ideal situation is to hide those negative emotions completely.

I wish that I could report that expressing your sadness, anxiety, frustration, and worries at work could be a good thing. But it's not. To benefit your career, it seems that the best thing to do is to conceal whatever negative emotions may be churning within you. If you're feeling disappointed, embarrassed, upset, or overwhelmed, try to pretend that you're not.

> To benefit your career, it seems that the best thing to do is to conceal whatever negative emotions may be churning within you.

But, if you do find your emotions getting the better of you – that you're venting your feelings in a public setting – then explain that you only feel this way because you are so incredibly passionate about your work. Say that your clients, your customers, your colleagues, or the work itself all just mean so much to you. And at least that way, you can regain some of your standing amongst your colleagues.

Publicly reframing distress as passion

Work can be incredibly stressful at times. But this advice is specifically about making your distress more palatable to your colleagues or clients. If you're fortunate enough never to show your sadness, frustration, or anxiety to others, then you won't need this.

Ideally, you would be able to keep your negative emotions completely hidden. But life isn't always ideal, is it? If you do ever let your emotions show in public, remember to explain your feelings in terms of how passionate you are – how much your work means to you or how much you care about your customers, for example.

And that's all there is to it. Do that and you help your colleagues to see you as competent and capable as opposed to lacking control over your emotions.

Learning to revalue and reframe your assets

Have you ever been bullied, harassed, or called pejorative names? Maybe people picked on you for your weight, your height, a mole on your face, your red hair, or something else about your appearance. Perhaps you're a woman who has been belittled or marginalized by men. Possibly you're disabled or you belong to an ethnic, religious, or cultural minority and you've had people be nasty to your face. Or you're part of the lesbian, gay, bisexual, trans, and queer community. Older people, younger people, folks who have experienced mental illness, as well as people of different social classes get mocked, too. And of course all of this can be downright stressful.

Just ask any black person who has been called the N word, a woman who has been labelled a 'bitch', or a gay man a 'queer'. Or perhaps you're an accountant, a software engineer, or IT consultant who gets brushed aside as a mere 'nerd' or 'geek'.

Some individuals as well as social groups advocate re-appropriating such labels. For example, rap stars often refer to themselves and their friends with derivatives of the N word. The American singer-songwriter Meredith Brooks released a song entitled 'Bitch', in which she triumphantly proclaims 'I'm a bitch.' And many gay activists endorse reclaiming the word 'queer' to turn it from an insult into a badge of pride.

Great idea. But does this self-labelling technique actually work?

A team led by Columbia University researcher Adam Galinsky recruited hundreds of individuals in a series of studies to explore this very question. And their results supported the re-appropriation of slurs. For example, in one experiment, they found that participants who had deliberately chosen to label themselves with such pejorative words said that they felt distinctly more powerful than other participants who simply thought back to times that they had been attacked in such ways. And in another experiment, onlookers said that they perceived self-labelling individuals as more powerful, too.[14]

The two pieces of evidence are important. Taking control by choosing to apply a negative label may not just help people to feel more powerful – it may also help them to appear more powerful in the eyes of others.

> Taking control by choosing to apply a negative label may not just help people to feel more powerful – it may also help them to appear more powerful in the eyes of others.

Taking ownership of slur terms

An old English adage says: 'Sticks and stones may break my bones, but words will never hurt me.' The implication is that physical attacks can cause pain and distress but mere words cannot. It's a lovely idea. But of course we know that isn't true. Because words *can* be hurtful.

If you feel stressed because people are insulting you with a slur, try self-labelling instead. Rather than trying to deny the word, make an attempt to reclaim the word. Use that label to refer to yourself. Take pride in your membership of that group and look at that group membership – being a woman, being of a different ethnicity, being gay, and so on – as something that gives you a unique perspective on the world and different strengths, too.

Simply remember the scientific research. People who recall times they self-labelled feel more powerful.

Onwards and upwards

- Remember that your level of stress matters at both the physiological and the psychological level. The more you feel stressed, the more likely you are to suffer from physical ill health and diseases ranging from colitis to heart disease. Tackling stress and helping yourself to feel better may have real benefits for your physical and mental health.

- To recover more quickly from stress, consider using the ecphory technique. Assemble whatever cues you like – photographs, objects which hold a special meaning to you, or even just words or phrases – that will allow you to trigger the retrieval of happy memories. I know that it sounds too easy. But rest assured that there's solid research showing it can help to calm both mental and physical symptoms of stress.

- When you have more time, invest in your continuing health by writing about your future and how you would like your life to turn out. It's not something that you can do in only a handful of minutes – it will probably take at least 10 to 20 or more minutes of your time. But remember that this one-off exercise has been shown to have benefits that kick in within only 48 hours and can last for at least three months.

- When you're at work, turn off your email notifications and check it less. Participants who checked their email only a handful of times a day reported feeling less stressed *and* more productive. They even said that they slept better.

- If your colleagues spot that you seem overwhelmed by your work, avoid telling them that you feel stressed or emotional. Instead, tell them how passionate you feel. This small change in phrasing may positively affect how your colleagues think about you.

- Finally, consider re-appropriating negative language that attackers may throw at you in their attempts to belittle or bully you. If you can take pride in your uniqueness, you can help yourself to feel and appear in others' eyes considerably stronger and more in charge.

2

Boosting your motivation and achieving your goals

'A goal without a plan is just a wish.'

Antoine de Saint-Exupéry

What would you most like to change about your life or yourself? Perhaps you want a promotion or a better job somewhere else. Maybe you want to be successful and financially secure. Or it could be that you want to find someone special – or to move on from an unhappy situation.

The change may be to do with how you think and feel about yourself. You wish you could be more confident, more creative, more energetic, more forgiving. Or maybe less impulsive, less scared, less angry, less distractible. Or your goal is about a specific behaviour: to spend less money, lose weight, learn a new language, quit smoking, or anything else.

We set goals because we want to be better in some way. However, the truth is that change isn't easy. Just think of all the people you know who have set New Year's resolutions only to give up on them by about the middle of February – if not sooner. Or you may have tried and failed in the past yourself, too.

But of course *some* people do manage to overhaul their lives. There are plenty of people who do lose massive amounts of weight, find love, overcome feelings of anxiety, run marathons, change careers, and so on. And psychological scientists have been quietly uncovering tweaks, exercises, and hacks that give people the very best shot at staying motivated and achieving their goals. For example, it turns out that it helps to start at the beginning, by thinking about the very nature and phrasing of your goals. So let's start there straightaway.

Start at the beginning, by thinking about the very nature and phrasing of your goals.

Pursuing what you want – not what you don't want

In terms of our physical health, there are so many goals that we *should* be pursuing in life. Most of us could do with cutting back on sugary snacks, alcohol, salt, and foods that contain processed trans fats. Warnings about skin cancer (and premature ageing) tell us that we should be wearing hats and generally staying out of the sun – or that we should at least be covering ourselves in sunscreen when the sun is shining. Most of us could benefit from doing more exercise, and maybe eating a few more vegetables and making it a habit to have oily fish a bit more often, too – oh, and definitely stopping smoking completely.

Broadly speaking, such goals can be divided into two categories: do's versus don'ts. But as psychologists like to be more specific about such things, we call them approach versus avoidance goals. In the technical language, approach goals are about striving towards a positive outcome; avoidance goals are about striving to get away from a negative outcome.

> Approach goals are about striving towards a positive outcome; avoidance goals are about striving to get away from a negative outcome.

Let's consider a couple of examples. Approach goals could include things like: 'Do more exercise' and 'Wear sunscreen when I'm sunbathing.' In contrast, avoidance goals include 'Don't smoke' and 'Don't drink alcohol on weekdays.'

Choosing an approach versus an avoidance goal is about deciding how you want to focus your attention. For example, suppose you want to save more money. Would it be a better idea to say, 'Do save more money every month' or 'Don't spend so much money'?

A classic experiment led by the University of Rochester's Andrew Elliot set out to answer this very question. The researchers recruited over a hundred high school students to take part in a problem solving test, consisting of 10 problems. The students were specifically told that their performance would be compared against those of their peers: 'The purpose of this study is to compare high school students with one another in their ability to solve these problems.'

Half of the students were then given an approach goal. They were told that the test was an opportunity for them 'to demonstrate that you are an exceptional problem solver'. The other half of the students were given an avoidance goal; they were told that the test would allow them 'to demonstrate that you are not a poor problem solver'.

The students were given just five minutes to complete the test. But that was enough time to see a clear difference in the performance of the two groups. Students who had been set an approach goal on average got 71% of the problems right. Their peers who had been set the avoidance goal performed much more poorly, only achieving scores of 58% on average.[1]

Clearly, setting an approach goal – to demonstrate that they were good problem solvers – helped students to do distinctly better. This small change in focus had measurable effects.

Now, I'm not saying that you will always get a 13% boost to your performance. However, the same effect has been replicated time and again, in a variety of situations. Take eating, for example. Researchers Meredith David from Baylor University and Kelly Haws from Vanderbilt University looked at the helpfulness of approach versus avoidance goals in changing people's eating patterns in order to be healthier.

The research duo asked participants to formulate either approach or avoidance goals with regards to what they should or shouldn't eat. Participants instructed to focus on approach goals were told to: 'List as many foods as you can think of that you should include and/or try to eat more of while you are on your diet. In other words, foods that are HELPFUL for dieting.' Participants told to set avoidance goals were required to 'List as many foods as you can think of that you should avoid and/or try to limit while you are on your diet. In other words, foods that are NOT helpful for dieting.'

It's not a difficult exercise. I'm sure you could quickly come up with your own lists of helpful or not helpful foods.

Cutting a long story short, the researchers found that setting approach goals tended to be more beneficial. Participants who listed foods that they should approach (e.g. carrots, apples, and broccoli) typically demonstrated more self-control than participants who wrote down foods that they should avoid (e.g. cake, French fries, and chocolate). It was only a small difference. But a measurable difference nonetheless.[2]

> Approach goals typically lead to better outcomes.

Why do approach goals typically lead to better outcomes? The food experiment researchers David and Haws suggested that trying to resist unhealthy foods might lead to an intense preoccupation with and desire for those forbidden foods. Think about it: if you're constantly reminding yourself *not* to eat cake, then you're actually spending a lot of time envisioning cake. And if you're thinking about avoiding cake so much of the time, you're still not giving yourself a more productive goal of

what you should be eating instead. It seems that the more successful tactic may instead be to focus on what you *can* consume:
apples, bananas, or breath mints, perhaps.

Striving for success rather than steering clear of problems

Broadly speaking, people who set approach goals tend to
accomplish more than those who set avoidance goals. Remember
that approach goals involve setting your sights on things you want
to achieve, whereas avoidance goals involve staying away from
unappealing or even harmful outcomes.

So how might you phrase your goals? If, for example, you're trying to
quit smoking, don't aim to 'Stop smoking cigarettes.' Aim to replace
it with a positive behaviour such as, 'Chew more gum' or 'Take three
sips of water' when you're craving a cigarette instead.

In your work or personal life, avoid goals such as, 'Don't be
impatient' or 'Don't say something stupid.' Try to focus your attention
on a more productive behaviour. You could try something like: 'Take
five deep breaths' or 'In meetings, ask for more time by saying: "Let
me think about that for a moment."'

One of my friends was recently diagnosed with skin cancer. This
prompted his wife to want to look after her skin, and initially she
decided to wear sunscreen to 'avoid getting burnt and risking
cancer'. However, I suggested another way of looking at it: why
not think about it as 'staying youthful' instead? She agreed that it
was a better way of thinking about it – and of course aiming to
retain her looks is more of an approach goal.

This doesn't mean that you should *never* set avoidance goals.
The science is not saying that avoidance goals are always inef-
fective. In terms of healthier eating goals, for example, David
and Haws merely report that 'although understanding the types
of behaviours (and foods) to avoid or minimize can be helpful,

the downsides of such a strategy suggest that it might be more difficult to implement and sustain effectively.' So avoidance goals may be 'more difficult' – but not impossible – to put into practice.

Anyway, you get the idea. If you can, aspire to achieve something positive rather than to avoid things that you fear or dislike.

> Aspire to achieve something positive rather than to avoid things that you fear or dislike.

Harnessing the power of empowered refusal

Have you ever been in a situation when friends or colleagues are trying to pressurize you to do something that isn't quite in keeping with your goals? They're teasing or tempting you, maybe because it suits them. For instance, perhaps you're trying to drink less alcohol but your colleagues are encouraging you to have just one more so that they'll feel less guilty about continuing to drink. Or you'd like to stay in to study but your friends want you to go out with them and have a good time instead.

In such situations, it isn't enough just to have goals that you keep to yourself. Sometimes, you may need to be able to communicate to other people exactly what you want – or don't want. And research tells us that yet another linguistic trick may help to strengthen your resolve.

> Sometimes, you may need to be able to communicate to other people exactly what you want – or don't want.

Scientists Vanessa Patrick from the University of Houston and Henrik Hagtvedt from Boston College have run several experiments looking at how people's use of language can help them to resist temptation. In one study, they taught a group of 20 adult women one of two strategies for staying on track.[3]

Half of the women were taught to resist whatever temptations came their way by using the word 'don't' (e.g. saying, 'I don't binge watch television', 'I don't eat sugary snacks', and 'I don't allow myself to be lazy.') The other half of the women were told to resist temptation by using the word 'can't' (e.g. saying, ' I can't binge watch television', 'I can't eat sugary snacks', and 'I can't allow myself to be lazy.')

Over the next 10 days, all of the women were invited to report daily on their progress using whichever verbal strategy they had been taught. And it transpired that there was a remarkable difference between the two tactics.

Eight of the participants who had been taught to resist temptation using the word 'don't' were still using the strategy on the tenth day. However, only one of the participants who had learnt to use the word 'can't' persisted with it to the tenth day – all of the other women had given up on it.

That's a massive difference, right? Using the word 'don't' was eight times as popular as using the word 'can't' to resist temptation.

Patrick and Hagtvedt wondered whether this was a robust effect. So they ran further experiments with different people and other scenarios. But they came up with similar results.

The research suggests that people who use the word 'don't' tend to feel more self-motivated and in charge – they feel as if they have made a positive, deliberate decision not to do something. In contrast, people who use the word 'can't' are implying that someone else – perhaps a partner, friends, family, colleagues, or society in general – is in charge. Using the word 'can't' makes people feel as if they are being forced against their will not to do something.

People who use the word 'don't' tend to feel more self-motivated and in charge. In contrast, people who use the word 'can't' are implying that someone else is in charge.

Saying 'no' from a place of strength

Research tells us that resisting temptation by saying 'I don't' is more psychologically empowering than using 'I can't'. So you can use this in a variety of ways.

Clearly, you can use it to refuse temptations that threaten to derail your goals. If you're trying to quit smoking, say to people, 'I don't smoke' rather than, 'I can't smoke.' It's more assertive. The implicit message you're sending when you say 'I don't' is that this refusal is part of your stable, unchanging, ongoing identity. In contrast, saying 'I can't' suggests that there's something or someone other than you that is preventing you from doing so and that you may be persuaded to break the rule if people pester you enough about it.

Using 'I don't' language works whether you are refusing temptation out loud to other people or just trying to boost your own resolve. For example, suppose you want to motivate yourself to study or go to the gym rather than sit on the sofa and watch Netflix. Tell yourself, 'I don't sit around watching Netflix – I'm going to study' rather than, 'I can't sit around watching Netflix – I'm going to study.'

Yes, it seems like a tiny linguistic difference. But psychological science tells us that it's a change that may boost your motivation just that little bit more and help you to stay on course towards your goals.

After learning about the principle of using 'don't' rather than 'can't' language, I often notice examples of it now. A couple of months ago, I worked with a client who told me that he no longer drinks alcohol because he is a recovering alcoholic. He didn't say that he 'can't' drink. When he said 'I don't drink', he was sending a very clear message that alcohol was not an option for him under any circumstances. And as a result, he had not had any alcohol for well over five years.

> Using 'I don't' language works whether you are refusing temptation out loud to other people or just trying to boost your own resolve.

Specifying when and how you want to succeed

So far I've been talking in rather broad terms about goals. But let's get more specific now about you – about your life and goals. What exactly do you want to achieve, change, or improve?

I'm going to tell you about a research experiment shortly. But if you would like to play along, you could try this short exercise. Your assignment is to spend 90 seconds coming up with as many goals as you like. The aim, though, is not to generate a massive list. The time limit is only to make this task quick and manageable.

Some of these goals may be fairly short-term – tasks you want to complete within the next few days or weeks, perhaps. Others may be projects that require longer timeframes over many months or even years. And to help you to generate your goals, use the following prompt:

In the future it will be important for me to...

Just for a minute and a half, remember. See what comes to mind.

Ready? Go.

In a recent study, Joanne Dickson at the University of Liverpool and her colleague Nicholas Moberly from the University of Exeter asked several dozen people to do a very similar exercise. Adults aged from 18 to 81 were given 90 seconds to list however many goals they liked.

There was a twist to the study, though. Roughly half of the participants were a broad range of adults drawn from local communities. The other half were adults who were being treated for mental health issues – specifically, they had been diagnosed with major depression. The researchers had a hunch that depressed people would have a different way of thinking about the goals they wanted to achieve in life.

The researchers initially counted the number of goals that the two groups produced and discovered that both generated more or less the same quantity of goals. The depressed participants had just as many goals as the non-depressed adults.

Suspecting that the difference would be to do with quality rather than quantity, the researchers then asked two expert judges to categorize each of the participants' goals as either specific or general. For example, specific goals might include: 'Do my ironing for next week', 'Go to the gym twice a week', and 'Save £500 by January.' In contrast, goals such as 'Keep the house tidier', 'Get fit', and 'Save more money' would be categorized as general in nature.

And it was this that differentiated the depressed from the non-depressed participants. The depressed participants tended to come up with a larger proportion of general goals and fewer specific ones.[4] While depressed people were able to come up with a similar number of ambitions overall, their goals tended to be broader, more ambiguous, and arguably more open to interpretation.

It's a result that hints at something intriguing. It suggests that depression may somehow be linked to a reduced ability to form specific goals.

But which is the cause and which the effect? Does the onset of depression make people less able to generate specific goals? Or does having vaguer goals make it more likely that people will fail to achieve them and then feel depressed?

Setting more specific goals rather than broad ones may help people to accomplish more.

If the latter is true, then it should be the case that setting specific goals rather than broad ones will help people to accomplish more. And this is precisely what University of Sheffield researcher Christopher Armitage set out to test. In particular, he wanted to answer the question: would setting a very specific goal help people to eat more healthily?

Armitage began by recruiting 120 students for what he told them was a university dietary study. All of the students were given a booklet of questions to complete. For example, they answered questions such as, 'To what extent do you see yourself as being capable of eating an extra piece of fruit each day in the next two weeks?' and 'How confident are you that you will be able to eat an extra piece of fruit each day in the next two weeks?'

Answering such questions of course made the students much more aware of their dietary habits. But Armitage had secretly divided the students into two groups. The first (control) group merely answered broad questions about their thoughts, beliefs, and feelings about eating more fruit. The second (experimental) group answered one additional question. Their questionnaire booklets told them:

> You are more likely to eat an extra piece of fruit each day if you decide when and where you will do so. Please write in the space below when and where you will eat an extra piece of fruit each day in the next two weeks.

That's a pretty small request, right? I'm sure it would take you no more than a few seconds to write down that kind of a goal.

Two weeks later, when the researcher asked all of the students to report how much fruit they had actually eaten, he noticed a whopping difference. While participants in the control group had on average eaten 8.2 pieces of fruit during that two-week period, participants in the experimental group reported that they had typically eaten 14.3 pieces of fruit.[5]

To me, that's a fairly impressive result. First of all, the difference between 8.2 and 14.3 is more than decent. But for me it's the fact that the intervention was so simple: merely asking participants to specify when and where they would eat an extra piece of fruit probably only took them a handful of seconds to do.

That really is a pretty small request, isn't it? You personally may or may not want to eat more fruit in your life. But just to see how this works, imagine now that you too would like to aim for an extra piece of fruit every day. See if you can figure out when and where would be best for you to gobble down an apple, banana, orange, or whatever else you might like to eat.

If you try it, an image probably pops into your head almost immediately. And remember in the study by Christopher Armitage that taking just a few seconds to write it down could make a marked difference.

Turning broad goals into specific actions

In psychological parlance, a goal that links a specific behaviour to a particular situation is called an implementation intention. Generally speaking, the format of an implementation intention needs to be: *If situation A occurs, then I will do B.* As a result, implementation intentions are also often called 'If… then…' goals.

For example, someone who wants to lose weight may write down a set of implementation intentions as follows:

- 'If I get home from work, then I will immediately walk up and down the stairs for five minutes.'

- 'If it's a Sunday, then I will go to the supermarket to buy a week's worth of apples, lettuce, butternut squash, sweet potatoes, green beans, avocados, and tomatoes for the fridge.'

- 'If Jessica asks me to share a dessert with her, then I will say, "You go ahead and have one by yourself if you like, but I'm just going to order a coffee, thanks."'

Someone else who wants to work towards a promotion at work may decide on these sorts of 'If… then…' statements:

- 'If it's the end of a working day, then I will review my progress and make a list of priorities for the next day.'

- 'If it's a Saturday morning, then I will spend an hour reading articles from *The Economist*, robyeung.com, and theguardian. com.'

- 'If it's the last Sunday in a month, then I will spend 30 minutes planning new learning activities for the coming month and I will write them up as implementation intentions.'

'If my boss asks me to do a project that doesn't help me get my next promotion, then I will ask for time to think about it and try to come up with a way of delegating it to someone else.'

I appreciate that the phrasing of these 'If… then…' goals may seem a bit awkward or unwieldy. But hopefully you can see that they can actually be used in just about any situation, whether you want to do something every day, every month, at certain times, or even with only particular people. And remember the bigger picture: that there is a robust body of evidence showing that they can be really beneficial in terms of boosting your motivation and giving you the very best shot at success.

There are literally thousands of studies showing the benefits of the 'If… then…' implementation intention format. It really is one of the most powerful techniques in psychological research.

I've written about them in several of my books, so I apologize if you have read one or more of my previous books and are thinking, 'But Dr Rob wrote about this in a couple of his other books!' I keep mentioning implementation intentions in new books not because I'm lazy or have run out of ideas to write about but because this is a truly powerful method. Once everyone I meet is telling me that they are using the 'If… then…' method, *that* is when I will stop writing about it.

Anyway, I'll leave you with a final thought. If you did the 90-second goal setting exercise at the start of this section, take a look back at the goals that you wrote down. If you scribbled down any broad, overly generalized goals, could you rewrite them as a number of highly specific implementation intentions?

> There are literally thousands of studies showing the benefits of the 'If… then…' implementation intention format.

Going backwards to move forwards

Quite a few of the people who come to me for coaching and advice do so because they want to get promoted. Take Hamish, for example. He was a 30-something finance manager working at a hospital with his sights set on getting a job as a finance director. During our first coaching session, he told me that he had applied for over 20 jobs during the last year or so. He got invited to a couple of interviews, but mostly he didn't hear anything back – he usually didn't even get an acknowledgement of his application.

We quickly established that he had a fair amount of work to do in order to achieve his goal. He needed to build his profile and reputation within the health sector by giving more presentations at conferences and other industry events. He also didn't have very good connections with the kinds of people who might help him, so he decided that he would set up regular breakfast and lunch meetings so that he could schmooze people one on one.

He realized that he had gaps in terms of his technical, financial experience, too, so he committed to pursuing particular assignments and projects at work. And in terms of actually applying for jobs, he needed to completely overhaul his CV and learn a different way of composing covering letters. He also had to write out full, prose answers to likely interview questions and rehearse them until he could talk about his experience and achievements confidently.

In total, we identified 14 tasks and projects – some of them smaller and some much larger – that he would need to complete in order to give him the best possible chance of securing a promotion. But in terms of working out a timetable of activities for the coming months, I suggested that he work backwards.

It was January when we first met. And he set himself an aggressive deadline: he wanted to be applying for further jobs by the end of September. So I suggested that he should begin by figuring out what he should be doing in September first. And then work backwards to August. Then to July, June, and so on.

Perhaps you're not interested in getting promoted. So let's play around with a different hypothetical goal. Imagine for a moment that you have enough cash to build a house, the perfect home for you and your family. How would you go about planning the project? Would you start at the beginning – perhaps by arranging to visit possible plots of land and completing the legal paperwork for the construction? Or would you start at the end, by thinking about how you would decorate and then furnish your new home?

Your first instinct may be to start at the beginning. But the latest studies about how to plan well suggest that it may actually be a better idea to work backwards, in reverse chronological order.

For example, a team of researchers led by Jessica Wiese, a doctoral student at Wilfrid Laurier University in Canada, ran four experiments in which they asked participants to plan a variety of projects either from start to finish or in reverse chronological order. Several hundred participants drew up plans for projects, such as organizing a date, completing a university assignment, and booking a holiday.

Across all of the experiments, the researchers found that the participants who engaged in backward planning were generally better off. These participants were more able to identify potential obstacles. They were more likely to break their overall goals down into important steps. And they were more accurate in estimating how long their projects would actually take to complete. In contrast, participants who engaged in forward planning were more likely to get their estimates wrong – they tended to underestimate how long their projects would take.[6]

> The latest studies about how to plan well suggest that it may actually be a better idea to work backwards, in reverse chronological order.

So if you're planning on how to achieve a goal, it may be smarter and more productive to plan your project backwards from finish to start. This trick may better help you to spot likely problems, map out the major stages of your undertaking, and more accurately gauge the proper timetable for everything you need to do.

But there's more. An even more recent paper in the prestigious journal *Psychological Science* compared the effects of forward versus backward planning in participants from the US, China, and Korea. Led by Jooyoung Park, a management researcher at Peking University HSBC Business School in China, the researchers found that participants who engaged in backward planning also reported feeling more motivated about their projects than those who formulated their plans in the more conventional fashion. As a result, the participants who worked out their plans in reverse actually got better results in the end, too.[7]

Backward planning sounds like an odd idea. But different studies using different tasks and projects and in different countries come to similar conclusions. Backward planning helps people to pull together more realistic timetables for their projects and boosts their motivation for actually getting everything done, too.

Going back to my client Hamish then, you can see why I suggested he plan his campaign to get a promotion in reverse order. And whatever your goals, you may be able to benefit from the more insightful planning and enhanced motivation that comes from adopting this unlikely method, too.

> Backward planning helps people to pull together more realistic timetables for their projects and boosts their motivation for actually getting everything done, too.

Planning from finish to start

Some goals in life may be relatively straightforward: you wouldn't need to spend much time formulating a detailed plan of action if you're only aiming to go to the gym twice a week or cut down on your alcohol intake. But when it comes to achieving some of the more complex goals in life – studying for a qualification, planning a wedding, changing career, starting a family, and so on – it may be worth taking more time to make a plan. And to give yourself the very best shot at achieving your goals, the science suggests that you should plan backwards: that you should work out the actions you need to take in reverse chronological order.

You could perhaps begin by making a long list of all of the actions that you think you may need to do in order to get to your end goal. In this initial stage, don't think about which ones come first or later on. Just get all of the steps down in a document.

Then think about slotting the various actions into your timetable in reverse order. The end date of course depends on the size and nature of your topic. Organizing a party for a dozen friends may only take a few days; finding a new job in a different country could take many, many months.

As you try to decide on the reverse order of tasks, it is likely that you will identify potential problems, obstacles, or other tasks that you need to do. But that's a good thing. Better to spot what may happen early on during the planning than for setbacks to hit you later on when time may be short.

You don't need to spend much longer on reverse chronological planning than on the conventional kind. But the academic research does suggest that you will get a significantly better result out of it.

Sustaining your motivation

So far in this chapter we've covered several tips and procedures to help you formulate your goals and plan on how you will achieve them. But now let's imagine that you're making good progress towards a particular goal. With the end in sight, do you think you're more likely to keep track of how much you have already accomplished or how far you still have to go?

To illustrate what I mean, let's consider a hypothetical situation. Imagine that you set yourself a goal to save £1,000 – perhaps for a holiday or some other luxury. That was some months ago and now you have managed to put aside £750. So here's the question: would you tend to focus on the fact that you're three-quarters of the way to your goal – or that you still have one-quarter that you have yet to save?

Psychologists distinguish between these two ways of thinking. And studies suggest that one of these modes of tracking progress may be more beneficial in keeping us motivated and accelerating our progress towards our goals in life.

The evidence comes from a research team led by Florida State University researcher Kyle Conlon, who monitored a group of over a hundred overweight adults as they embarked on a 12-week weight loss programme. The participants were randomly assigned to one of three groups.

The first group was asked to adopt a so-called accomplishment focus; they were told to think about the weight that they managed to lose each week. The second group was instructed to adopt what's known as a goal focus by tracking how much weight they still needed to lose in order to achieve their overall weight loss goals. Participants in the third (control) group were given no further instructions on how they should think about their progress.

At the end of the 12 weeks, the researchers found that the participants who had been told to focus on what they had accomplished lost on average 2.7% of their body weight. However, the participants who had focused on their goals – i.e. on the gap between where they were and what they ultimately wanted to achieve – had dropped 4.6% of their body weight.[8]

Meanwhile, the control group, who had been given no specific instructions on how to track their progress, lost only 2.2% of their body weight. In other words, participants who focused on the gap made the greatest progress towards their goals.

Clearly, a goal focus is a more successful strategy than an accomplishment focus when tracking progress. But why?

Conlon and his colleagues suggested that people who focus on what they have achieved so far may feel more satisfied. And that sense of satisfaction with their progress may lead to a bit of complacency and therefore reduced motivation to keep pushing on. In contrast, people who concentrate on what they have yet to achieve stay slightly dissatisfied and (metaphorically) hungrier to achieve more. So their niggling sense of dissatisfaction may fire up their motivation just that little bit more.

> A goal focus is a more successful strategy than an accomplishment focus when tracking progress.

The implication is that there's a trade-off between contentment and motivation. If you're content, you may slacken off. If you focus on what you have yet to achieve, you help yourself to stay motivated. For example, imagine for a moment that you're an athlete and have won a bronze medal at the Olympic Games. Adopting an accomplishment focus, you may say to yourself: 'Wow, it's amazing that I've beaten dozens and dozens of people. I'm really grateful and lucky to have achieved so much in my life.' But if you want to spur yourself on, then you may be better off focusing on those two individuals who beat you and thinking something like: 'I need to get better than those two other people. I need to work harder in order to become the Olympic champion!'

Keeping your mind on the gap

The research suggests that focusing on what you have yet to achieve may be more motivating than focusing on what you have already achieved. This mode of thinking is about looking forwards to what you still need to do in the future rather than looking back and congratulating yourself on the progress of the recent past.

So if you're trying to save and put aside a certain sum of money, focus on what you have not saved rather than what you have. If you're studying for an exam, keep reminding yourself of the topics you still need to learn about rather than the ones you have already covered.

Of course, many goals do not have one end point. For example, you may be trying to adopt a new lifelong habit such as flossing your teeth. If you want to floss your teeth twice a day, that's 14 times a week. So when you manage nine times in a particular week, tell yourself that you still have five more to go before you can congratulate yourself on a truly successful week.

Focusing on what you have yet to achieve may be more motivating than focusing on what you have already achieved.

Onwards and upwards

- In deciding on your goals, remember the distinction between approach and avoidance goals. Broadly speaking, approach goals involve striving towards something that you want; avoidance goals involve trying to prevent outcomes that you don't want. Avoidance goals may be useful at times. But as a rule of thumb, you may find approach goals easier to achieve and sustain over time.

- Bear in mind that there is a vast body of research showing that people who set specific goals are much more likely to achieve them than people who set overly broad goals. Whatever your overall goal, be sure to turn it into a number of specific implementation intentions using the 'If… then…' format.

- When thinking through how you will achieve a larger or more challenging goal, consider using the backward planning method. Begin by thinking about the future end point and work in reverse chronological order to the present moment. You will be better able to identify possible issues and obstacles. And you'll be less at risk of underestimating the true timescale for your project, too.

- Finally, keep track of your progress by focusing your attention on what you have yet to achieve rather than what you have accomplished so far. This subtle shift in attitude is likely to fuel your motivation and help you to get better results in the long run.

3

Being smart about health and weight loss

'Every man is the builder of a temple, called his body.'

Henry David Thorcau

I've spent a fair chunk of my career working on and off in health and fitness. I qualified and worked as a gym instructor when I was doing my first (undergraduate) degree in psychology. Then I spent three years completing a doctorate in sport and exercise psychology, looking into ways to motivate people to exercise more.

Even these days, I still continue to give presentations and seminars on the psychology of health and fitness. And some of my clients want help with their health and weight. After all, our minds and bodies are not separate things. A smart, productive, happy mind has to reside in a strong, rested, healthy body.

One client initially asked me to coach him because he wanted to find a new job. Several years previously, Leon had been lured by a good salary and the promise of exciting work to become a human resources manager within a massive international company.

But he had quickly come to hate it. The hours had been extremely long and the nature of the work much more bureaucratic than he had expected.

When we met, he wasn't motivated to get in touch with recruitment consultants or to apply for jobs. And we soon discovered the mental blockage. He felt demotivated and ashamed of himself because he had put on a lot of weight. He worked 10-hour days, which meant he didn't have the time or energy to exercise. He felt constantly tired so ended up ordering takeaways laden with calories. And he drank a bottle of wine most evenings to numb himself after his tedious day at work.

He felt sufficiently dispirited about his weight that he had begun to lose his sex drive, too. And he didn't want to meet up with ex-colleagues or recruitment consultants that he knew because he was certain that they would be secretly judging him because of his size.

So we changed our plans. Rather than focusing exclusively on his job hunt, we would aim to get him fitter, healthier, and leaner, too.

We started small. For example, he had been eating almost no fruit or vegetables. So every morning he stopped at his favourite coffee shop and bought an apple or a banana to go with his latte. It took no extra time out of his day. But it meant that he was eating one portion of fruit every day almost immediately.

Another little change: he started going for a walk on Friday evenings. After work, he resolved to walk a mile before getting on his usual train to go home.

Many of the changes we introduced were common sense. But I presented him with a handful of psychological tactics too: he wrote in depth about his values and why his health mattered to him. He wrote down specific goals to achieve either daily or weekly. And he trained himself to eat as an activity on its own, rather than something to do while he was scrolling on his phone or watching Netflix.

Within months, the changes were evident. The softness of his jawline started to disappear. In conversation, he became more animated in the use of his arms. He spoke more quickly. He exuded energy. And of course he looked slimmer, too.

Many people want to better themselves by losing weight, getting fitter, or generally improving their health. But many techniques have been shown to have real benefits: 6% here, 9% there. Another 5% elsewhere. And it all adds up.

Many people struggle with losing weight, getting fitter, or generally improving their health.

In Chapter 2, we looked at how to boost your motivation and give you the best shot at achieving goals of all sorts. But in this chapter, we'll look at a half-dozen easy tricks and tips that have been shown to be beneficial, specifically in terms of your health, weight, and fitness.

Getting value out of values

Imagine you're reading an article about the risks of a sedentary lifestyle and why you should exercise more. The article starts off by saying, 'You are at risk. A sedentary lifestyle increases the risk of developing diabetes, hypertension, colon cancer, depression and anxiety, obesity, and weak muscles and bones.'

Scary stuff, right? But then the piece goes on to add: 'The more you sit, the more damage it does to your body. When you sit for long periods of time, your body can't handle sugar and fat – this can mean a higher risk for disease.'

Would you continue to read the article? Or would you simply flip the page and read something else a bit cheerier?

Researchers have known for some time that many health messages – to exercise more, eat more healthily, wear sunscreen, quit smoking, and so on – go unheeded. Often, when people are faced with messages that feel threatening, they just choose to think about something less frightening. But a group of researchers led by the University of Pennsylvania's Emily Falk have found that it's possible to make people much more receptive to messages to live more healthily.

> Often, when people are faced with messages that feel threatening, they just choose to think about something less frightening.

Falk and her colleagues recruited several dozen adults into a study on health and brain activity. At the very start of the study, the participants were presented with a list of eight values (creativity, friends and family, independence, humour, politics, religion, money, spontaneity) and asked to rank them in order of importance to them.

Half of the participants were then told to think about their highest ranked value and what it meant for them. For example, someone who said 'independence' mattered the most was asked to think further about only this topic. The other half of the participants were asked a question that had nothing to do with their values (specifically, they were asked to consider a situation when they might check the weather).

All of the participants were next instructed to read 50 statements about the dangers of a sedentary lifestyle along with tips on how to become more physically active. In fact, the two statements you read at the start of this section are lifted directly from those used by Falk and her collaborators.

That was the end of the psychological bit of the experiment. But before the participants left, they were all asked to wear accelerometer devices on their wrists which would measure objectively how much physical activity they each performed.

Over a four-week period, the scientists found a clear difference between the two groups. The experimental participants who had mulled over their highest ranked value ended up being significantly more active than the control participants who had pondered the weather.[1]

That's a good result: ranking a list of eight values and then thinking about the top value led to more physical activity. But there's even more: the researchers also used fMRI brain scanning equipment to monitor all of the participants as they read the

50 statements about health and exercise. And they found that the values exercise actually caused a different pattern of activation in the brain, particularly in something called the ventromedial prefrontal cortex (VMPFC), which is the brain region that processes thoughts about our own self-worth.

In other words, the values exercise changes something in the brain, which better allows us to take on board health messages. In turn, this enhanced receptivity to those messages may help us to achieve real change.

> The values exercise changes something in the brain, which better allows us to take on board health messages.

Most of us probably already know the kinds of behaviours we could do (or stop doing) in order to be healthier. Consume fewer processed foods. Eat more vegetables. Exercise more. Drink less alcohol. Wear sunscreen when we go out in the sun. Quit cigarettes entirely. Etcetera. The problem is not that we don't *understand* intellectually what to do. It's more often the case that we simply don't like the messages we're hearing. Perhaps we're too lazy to do what we know we're supposed to be doing. Or we enjoy eating chocolate bars, drinking beer and glasses of wine, and so on. And when we don't like these messages or feel threatened by them, we choose to ignore them.

However, the study by Falk and her fellow scientists tells us that thinking about our most cherished values in life could make messages about our bodies and health become more relevant and valuable. It may allow such messages to blast past our excuses and rationalizations to penetrate more deeply into our brains. And that could literally be life-changing.

Harnessing your core values to change your life

The research suggests that the values exercise may be most useful when you are trying to give serious consideration as to how you might go about changing your life and becoming healthier. So use this technique when you are perhaps reading about what you could be doing or actually trying to make a plan as to what you intend to change.

To boost your self-worth and hopefully encourage healthier behaviour, begin by considering the following eight values: creativity, friends and family, humour, independence, money, politics, religion, and spontaneity.

Write the numbers 1 to 8 down on a sheet of paper. Then try to rank the eight values from 1 (most important) to 8 (least important).

Next, consider your number 1 value. And write a short essay – just a few paragraphs – about that top value. Specifically, think about two points:

● Why is your number 1 value of such importance to you?

● And, describe a time when this most important value might give you a purpose in life.

Remember that the values exercise should be used as a precursor. So after you have completed the values exercise, be sure to spend some time reading about how you could change your health and life for the better. Read a book or magazine on the topic by a reputable expert; or perhaps go online to consult the latest thinking on the subject. Even better, make notes and create a plan for how you will actually do things differently from now on.

Rank your values. Write about your most cherished value. Then make a plan. That's essentially what this first section of this chapter has been about. But if you need inspiration about the kind of plan you should be making, then read on. Because our very next section looks at a method for creating precisely this kind of plan.

Rank your values. Write about your most cherished value. Then make a plan.

Strengthening your identity

I worked with a client, a 50-something-year-old manager, who came to me because he was suffering from a general sense of malaise in his career as well as his broader life. A major reason for his lack of drive was due to his sense that he was being unfairly disregarded by some of his colleagues. However, it didn't help that he wasn't looking after his health. For instance, he could get through most days without eating a single portion of fruit or vegetables.

One problem was that he didn't really like fruit. He didn't like most vegetables either. Except for baked beans. He liked tinned baked beans – especially when he mixed them with either sweetcorn or peas.

OK, we can work with that, I told him. So I encouraged him to think of himself as a 'bean eater'. And that was essentially all it took to trigger a period of healthier eating for him.

In terms of your health, what would you say your primary goal is? You may have more than one goal, but let's stick with your main one for now. Maybe you want to lose weight – or gain weight and build muscle. Or perhaps you too want to increase your vegetable consumption or achieve something different: cut down on sugar, drink more water or eat less meat, for example.

Whatever your goal, psychological research says that you can help yourself to accomplish it by changing your identity. To get the process started, just start telling yourself that from now on you want to become a 'weight loser', 'muscle builder', 'sugar avoider', 'water drinker' – or even a 'bean eater'.

> Whatever your goal, psychological research says that you can help yourself to accomplish it by changing your identity.

The research in question comes from the minds of Amanda Brouwer of Winona State University and Katie Mosack from the University of Wisconsin–Milwaukee, who set out to change the eating patterns of 124 women. A third of the women were put through a short educational programme to teach them about healthy eating. Another third were given the same educational programme but in addition were asked to create a label for themselves – calling themselves things like 'smaller portion eater', 'fruit includer', or 'less butter consumer'. And the final third of the participants were given no instruction on how they should change their lives.

All of the participants in the experiment kept food diaries for four weeks. And the researchers found that the educational programme about healthy eating had been a complete flop, a massive failure: the participants in this group ended up eating no more healthily than those who had been given no advice.

However, the participants who had created labels for themselves were by the end of the four weeks eating significantly more healthily than all of their other peers. In other words, coming up with seemingly silly names such as 'homemade meal maker' and 'water instead of pop drinker' made a measurable difference to their eating patterns and health.[2]

Why does this work? Because labels matter to people in lots of areas of their lives. For example, English people sometimes think of themselves as 'English' and at other times as 'British'. And while people from Scotland may think of themselves as 'Scottish' or sometimes 'British', they would never, ever describe themselves as 'English'.

Consider labels that people apply to themselves such as 'professional', 'extravert', 'parent', 'Christian', 'environmentally friendly', 'recovering alcoholic', and 'vegan'. Choosing such words often allows people to define themselves and strengthen their resolve to act in certain ways.

Think too about people who describe themselves as 'film fans', 'animal lovers', or 'computer gamers'. Or 'beer drinkers', 'live action role-players', or 'opera goers'. You would expect someone who feels an affinity with any of these groups to behave in certain ways, too.

Personally, I very much think of myself as a 'gym goer'. And I literally turn down social engagements in order to make sure that I can get to the gym sometimes two but usually three times a week.

The labels that we voluntarily attach to ourselves can affect our identity: the groups, gangs, or clubs that we mentally choose to associate with. And by strengthening the labels or identities in our minds, it seems that we can deliberately steer how we go on to behave.

So let's bring things back to your health and lifestyle goals again. What label might you apply to yourself?

> By strengthening the labels or identities in our minds, it seems that we can deliberately steer how we go on to behave.

Thinking of yourself as a 'doer'

The study by Brouwer and Mosack looked at healthy eating. But other research – for example by University of Missouri-Columbia duo Linda Houser-Marko and Kennon Sheldon – has also shown that the technique benefits people with sports and exercise goals, too.[3]

To begin, write down your healthy eating or activity goals. Whether you want to lose or gain weight, cut down on certain foods, or eat more of them, just write down a sentence that encapsulates what you'd like to achieve.

Next, look at what you've written and turn it into a 'doer' phrase. In other words, try to find a noun, a label, or category that you could apply to what you're trying to do. For example, if you want to exercise more, you could call yourself an 'exerciser' or 'gym goer'. Some people might like more idiosyncratic phrases such as 'gym bunny' or 'gym rat'. Or make up something completely new that encapsulates how you feel: 'fitness follower', 'bike rider', 'treadmill runner', or whatever you like. It just has to end with the suffix '-er'.

When you've done that, picture yourself being the phrase – the category or name – that you've chosen. What would that look and feel like? Once you've thought about it, write a few sentences explaining the kinds of behaviours that a 'gym goer' or 'bike rider', or whatever else your label is, might do. For example, you might decide to 'do two sets of 12 crunches', 'keep moving for 15 minutes', 'burn 180 calories on the stationary bike', or anything else you like.

Ultimately, you are aiming to create a handful of behaviours or actions (between two and five) that you are pledging to take in order to keep your newfound identity alive. So do whatever works for you.

Remember that your identity can be as individualistic as you are. My client liked the notion of being a 'bean eater'. If you want to be a 'fizzy drink avoider' or 'croissant quitter' or 'real food instead of processed food eater', then go for it. If you decide that you like the idea of becoming a 'dairy disallower' or 'chocolate circumventor', then so what if it's not good English?

Embrace an identity that means something to you – you don't have to share it with anyone else unless you really want to. This is about finding a phrase that encourages you to change your behaviour in whatever ways you like. So do what works for you.

Embrace an identity that means something to you – you don't have to share it with anyone else unless you really want to.

Channelling the power of your imagination

Have you ever overeaten and regretted it? The last time I did that was maybe six months ago, when I went to a friend's dinner party. Kay had invited three friends to watch a movie (the Oscar-nominated ice skating biopic *I, Tonya*) at her home and we each contributed food items to share. Richard brought a large box of Lindt chocolates. Tilly arrived with a dozen exquisite chocolate cupcakes. I brought several large bags of toffee popcorn. And Kay roasted chicken pieces in garlic oil and served them with chilli-infused broccoli on the side.

I ate a huge amount. I had several chicken pieces with a good helping of broccoli. Then I had seconds of that. I had two cupcakes, plus maybe a half-dozen chocolates. And probably the equivalent of an entire bag of the toffee popcorn – that alone was around 800 calories. Basically, I most likely consumed around two to three times as many calories in that one sitting as I should have done. I felt seriously bloated for several hours afterwards and kept thinking that it would take me hours at the gym to burn off the sugar calories alone.

If you are ever concerned about overeating and want to curb your appetite – whether it's for junk food or anything else –

you may want to take notice of a study published in the top academic journal *Science*. A team of researchers led by Carey Morewedge, a social scientist at Carnegie Mellon University, essentially found that simply imagining eating a desired food may help people to rein in their consumption.

> Simply imagining eating a desired food may help people to rein in their consumption.

The researchers began by recruiting 51 experimental participants with a rather tempting offer: to eat as many M&M chocolates as they wanted to. However, all of the participants were first divided into three groups. Each group was then instructed to spend a few minutes imagining one of three scenarios:

- Inserting 33 coins into a laundry machine.
- Inserting 30 coins into a laundry machine and then eating 3 M&Ms.
- Inserting only 3 coins into a laundry machine but then eating 30 M&Ms.

The participants then helped themselves to as many M&Ms as they wanted to eat. The researchers simply counted how many each person ate.

Just looking at the design of the study, it's hard to work out what the researchers were trying to do. But hidden amongst those three groups was an ingenious experiment.

The main finding from the study was that participants who imagined eating more M&Ms went on to eat fewer of them. In some cases, people who imagined that they had eaten 30 M&Ms ended up eating nearly half as many as participants who had imagined the other scenarios.

As I said, the design of the experiment was rather clever – and here's why. The researchers could have created three conditions in which participants merely imagined consuming 30, 3, or 0 M&Ms. But then that could have opened the results of the study up to criticism. Perhaps simply engaging in *any* lengthy act of mental imagination could curb people's appetite. But by getting participants to imagine inserting 33 coins into a laundry machine (a physical act which isn't too dissimilar to inserting M&Ms into a mouth), the researchers were able to rule out this alternative explanation.

The researchers also repeated the experiment with a savoury food (chunks of cheese) and again found that participants who imagined eating lots of cubes of cheese went on to eat less cheese. In fact, based on five different studies, the researchers reliably demonstrated that merely imagining eating a food – whether sweet or savoury – may curb people's actual consumption of it.[4]

> Merely imagining eating a food – whether sweet or savoury – may curb people's actual consumption of it.

So if I had merely imagined eating mouthful after mouthful of toffee popcorn, I could have slashed the amount that I ended up eating. Oh well. I now know better for next time. And now, so do you.

For me, this study and its findings are a reminder that the human imagination is astonishingly powerful. And simply imagining that we have eaten something may help to persuade our stomachs that we actually have.

Best of all, this is such an easy intervention. You can do it any-time and anywhere. So if you want to cut down the amount you will eat – perhaps at a party or an all-you-can-eat buffet – simply spend a few minutes imagining the kinds of foods you will eat. The more you imagine eating the food, the less you may crave it. And you may ultimately eat less too.

I already know when I am going to use this next. I'm most likely to gorge on toffee popcorn at the cinema. When I go to see the latest action movie or Marvel superheroes film, I usually buy an enormous bag of toffee popcorn and eat it all by myself. But perhaps during the adverts I could spend a minute performing a mental simulation of eating popcorn. That should help to curb my appetite when I eventually do open the actual bag of popcorn to begin eating it.

Switching off to switch on satiety

Using the imagination to create mental simulations – movies in our minds – of ourselves eating may help to curb our actual appetite. But it turns out that movies and TV shows in the real world may sort of have the reverse effect.

But before we get into the effects of television on our eating habits, let's delve into the psychology of TV a bit further. For example, did you know that television can act as a painkiller? In one famous study, researchers found that children who were having blood taken from veins in their arms reported experiencing significantly less pain when watching television. In fact, children – in this study aged between 7 and 12 years – found cartoons a more effective method of reducing pain than having their mothers in the room speaking, caressing, or otherwise trying to soothe them.[5]

You're probably not surprised by that. We've all experienced that television can be mesmerizing, fun, and sometimes intensely engaging. So it makes sense that it can take people's minds off the pain of having big needles shoved into their arms.

> Television can be mesmerizing, fun, and sometimes intensely engaging.

Following this line of thinking, psychological scientists Lucy Braude and Richard Stevenson at Macquarie University in Australia wondered: might television also have a distracting effect on people while they eat? Now, you could argue it either way. Watching television might potentially help people to eat less because TV might distract them from their food. Or watching television might make people eat more because they don't notice that their stomachs are actually full.

Before we get to the science bit, which theory do you think is the more likely?

Of course, the only way to test the effects of television on eating would be to run an experiment. So the research duo recruited young adults to eat snacks while either watching a full 20-minute episode of the classic TV show *Friends* or simply sitting quietly for the same length of time.

And guess what? The participants who snacked while watching TV ate a *lot* more. Participants who were given the opportunity to eat as much as they liked without TV consumed 100 calories of snacks. Those who watched TV wolfed down 156 calories.[6]

Remember, too, that was only while watching one 20-minute TV show. Just imagine the damage you could do while bingeing on a boxset.

If those results could be replicated in other situations, that would be an astonishing difference. Simply switching off the television might help people to consume 36% less calories.

The researchers also looked at the effects of TV versus no TV on four different types of snacks – two sugary snacks, one healthy snack (almonds), and one salted snack (potato chips) – and found similar results. With every type of food, experimental participants who watched TV ate significantly more calories than those who just sat with no distractions for the same length of time.

And it's not just funny television shows like *Friends* that cause overeating either. A separate study led by psychological scientist Dolly Mittal found that sad or boring as well as funny TV shows all led to more overeating than not watching TV at all.[7] Unfortunately, then, the fairly inescapable conclusion from these multiple studies is that watching TV encourages most people to munch, chomp, guzzle, and devour more food.

> Watching TV encourages most people to munch, chomp, guzzle, and devour more food.

Why?

Other studies suggest that watching television while eating interferes with our ability to notice when we are full: we are less able to detect when we are satiated, so we end up overeating. That may sound ridiculous, but remember that television is so potent a form of distraction that it can soothe people and reduce the physical pain of having large needles pushed into the body.

The implication is clear then: TV is bad news if you're trying to be good about your eating. So switch off the television to switch on your satiety receptors – it will allow your brain to detect more quickly when you're full and you'll avoid overeating. Or to put it in really simple terms: if you want to lose weight, don't watch TV while you're eating.

Switch off the television to switch on your
satiety receptors.

Enjoying the sounds of scoffing

TV isn't the only thing that can make you overeat. You probably won't be surprised to hear that people tend to eat and
drink more when music is playing.[8] But the latest research suggests that simply being in a noisier environment may make you
eat more without you realizing it, too.

Marketing researchers Ryan Elder from Brigham Young University and Gina Mohr of Colorado State University invited 67
young men and women to eat as many pretzels as they liked.
Each participant was sitting in front of a plain white bowl filled
with pretzels. Oh, and the participants had to wear headphones
while they ate.

The researchers played moderately loud background noise
through the headphones to half of the participants – just loud
enough to cover up the sound of the participants' munching
and crunching. The researchers also played background noise to
the other half of the participants – but at a much quieter level.

On average, the participants who listened to the louder background noise ate 4.1 pretzels each. Participants who listened to
the much quieter background noise chose to eat only 2.8 pretzels. In other words, noisier environments – or even background
music – could potentially encourage overeating.

I know that the difference between 2.8 pretzels and 4.1 pretzels may not seem like a lot in absolute terms. But let's look at
it instead in percentage terms: participants who heard louder
background noise ate a whopping 46% more. That could seriously add up over time.

To further investigate the effects of sounds on overeating, the research partners continued by running a slightly different experiment. This time, they gave participants the opportunity to eat as many cookies as they wanted. However, the participants were actually split into three groups, each of which was given a different set of instructions as to how they should eat:

- 'We would like you to eat the snack food as loudly as you can.'

- 'We would like you to eat the snack food as quietly as you can.'

- 'We would like you to eat the snack food as you ordinarily would.'

Once again, the researchers totalled up the numbers of cookies that each participant consumed. They counted that participants told to eat as they would do ordinarily ate 3.4 cookies. But participants who were told to focus on either eating loudly or quietly ate discernibly less (2.6 cookies, on average).[9]

In absolute terms, that also does not appear to be a huge difference. But going from eating 3.4 cookies to 2.6 cookies is actually a 24% reduction. And it came about by pointing out to participants that they should focus on the sounds of their eating. It didn't matter whether they were asked to eat more loudly or quietly. It had the same effect: it encouraged them to eat less.

Taking both the pretzel and cookie studies together, then, it seems as if background sounds and noises may encourage overeating because they distract us from the sounds of our own munching. When we are able to hear – or instructed to pay attention to – the sound of our eating, it acts as what Elder and Mohr call a 'consumption monitoring cue'. We simply become more aware of our eating and how much we feel we should allow ourselves to eat. As a result, we may end up eating less.

> The sound of our eating acts as a 'consumption monitoring cue'.

It's a trick that I apply within my own life. I love chocolate and like most cakes. But one of my favourite indulgences is a chocolate brownie. When I meet friends and chat while eating – perhaps in a buzzy coffee shop – I always finish the whole brownie.

When I buy one to eat at home, though, I cut the brownie up into six pieces and just sit with the plate in front of me. No TV. No radio or Spotify. I eat slowly, relishing every bite as the chocolatey, sugary, buttery flavours fill my mouth. The first few pieces are intensely enjoyable, delightful, satisfying. But without distractions, I usually notice that I've had enough after five or sometimes just four pieces. So I throw the rest away, probably saving myself a hundred or more calories in the process.

Of course, you're free to eat however you like. But if you do wish to avoid overeating, consider not just turning off the TV but also eating in a quiet environment so that you can focus fully on the sounds of your own scoffing.

Altering your attitude to boost your health and happiness

We all know that physical exercise is good for us, right? Even just walking for 10 minutes can trigger a host of benefits for our minds as well as bodies. And over time, few would doubt that physical exercise can make us leaner, stronger, healthier, and even sexier.

But the problem is that we don't always feel like exercising. Sometimes we feel that we're too busy to exercise. Other times, we feel lazy. Perhaps the weather is cold and wet or scorchingly hot – and the prospect of putting on trainers to do any physical exercise just isn't terribly appealing. But I'm going to introduce you to a little mental trick that may allow you to adjust your mental outlook so that you feel more motivated to get moving.

To delve into this mental attitude, let me ask you two questions. To what extent do you feel that you have much in life to be thankful for? And to what degree are you grateful to a wide variety of people?

The more you feel thankful and grateful, the higher your level of dispositional gratitude, which psychologists have defined as a psychological orientation towards noticing and appreciating the positive in life. Personally, I feel that I have so much to be thankful for: loving parents, a supportive and self-effacing partner, a comfortable home, friends with a similar outlook on life, work that I (usually) genuinely enjoy, and clients who are easy-going yet appreciative. And when I read about world events and conflicts, I am thankful to be living in a democracy in which I have so much freedom of choice and expression.

Research has found that dispositional gratitude may drive people to do more exercise and look after themselves better. Major evidence to support this comes from a study carried out in a group of 962 Swiss adults aged between 19 and 84 years of age. In addition, those who felt more grateful about their lives also reported being in better physical health.[10]

> Dispositional gratitude may drive people to do more exercise and look after themselves more.

From a strictly scientific perspective, the study only tells us that gratitude and physical exercise are linked. But do you just have a certain level of gratitude that is fixed and unchangeable? Or is it possible to improve your level of gratitude – and therefore boost how much exercise you do, too?

For the answers to such questions, we turn to a classic study conducted by Robert Emmons from the University of California, Davis, and Michael McCullough from the University of Miami. The pair of academic psychologists recruited 192 undergraduate students into a study looking at the effects of different psychological exercises on their mental and physical health. The participants were divided into three groups, with each group asked to complete a short written assignment once a week, every week for 10 weeks.

The first group were asked to recall and write down up to five positive things in life that they felt grateful for. A second group were asked to write down up to five hassles – negative events or circumstances that annoyed or bothered them. Participants in the third group were asked to write down neutral events or circumstances that affected them.

After 10 weeks, participants who had completed the gratitude assignment reported multiple benefits. For a start, they felt significantly more positive about life. They reported feeling better about their lives as a whole; they were also more optimistic about the things they had to do in the near future. In other words, they were happier.

But there were also other, unexpected benefits from the gratitude assignment. The participants who completed the weekly written gratitude exercise said that they experienced fewer physical symptoms and ailments. And they also ended up doing nearly 1.5 hours more exercise than those participants who had listed their weekly hassles and gripes about life.[11]

In other words, the study by Emmons and McCullough demonstrates that it is possible to change your level of gratitude, with
multiple knock-on effects. You could feel happier. You may feel
physically healthier. And you could end up doing more exercise,
too. Isn't that a win–win–win situation?

Boosting your health and activity by developing your gratitude

There are many things in our lives, both large and small, that we may
be grateful about. And studies from several groups of researchers
have found that it's possible to focus more intently on these things
by completing a straightforward written assignment. Once a week,
simply write down up to five things in your life that you are grateful or
thankful for.

It's completely up to you what you write, but previous participants
have listed things as wide-ranging as 'my morning cup of coffee',
'the generosity of friends', 'my wonderful parents', 'waking up this
morning', and 'God, for giving me determination.'

And that's it. A written exercise that should only take you a couple of
minutes a week.

Now, the research did not find that participants became totally
ecstatic, completely healthy, and inexorably motivated to perform massive amounts of exercise. They only experienced
measurable improvements in all three areas as opposed to being
utterly transformed. However, you may still be wondering
how such a relatively humble exercise could produce so many
benefits.

Perhaps the answer lies in the fact that gratitude seems to
change what happens in the brain itself. For example, a recent
study led by Prathik Kini at Indiana University used fMRI

scanners to investigate precisely this issue. A group of participants performed a different gratitude exercise for 20 minutes, once a week for three weeks. When the scientists scanned the brains of the participants three months later, they observed a greater level of neural activity in the medial prefrontal cortex.[12]

> Gratitude seems to change what happens in the brain itself.

Yes, performing gratitude exercises totalling just 60 minutes resulted in changes in the brain that were measurable at least three months later. To me, that's pretty powerful stuff.

Anyway, I don't know about you. But personally I'm very grateful for the gratitude exercise.

Onwards and upwards

- Whether you want to improve your health or fitness, begin by writing about your most cherished value. Write a handful of paragraphs about this value in order to strengthen your resolve and set you up for making positive changes in your life.

- Further bolster your determination to change by applying a new 'doer' label (or labels) to yourself and your behaviour. Choose a noun or category that encapsulates what you are trying to achieve. Remember that this can be as idiosyncratic as you like – there can be no wrong answer here so long as it works for you. Then work out what actions you should take to make your new label(s) come to life.

- To stave off cravings for an unhealthy food, spend a minute imagining that you are eating mouthful after mouthful of it. Whether you are hankering after a sweet or savoury food, remember that this simple mental exercise could help to curb your actual appetite for it.

- To avoid overeating, turn off the TV. Television is such a potent form of distraction that it may override the ability of your body's built-in satiety receptors to detect when you've had enough to eat.

- Trust also research showing that even background noise may encourage overeating. Being able to hear the sounds of your own crunching and munching acts as a consumption monitoring cue. If you really want to avoid overeating, consider that it is better to focus your full attention on your eating – away from music, conversation, and other distractions.

- Boost both your mental and physical health by adopting a more grateful view of the positive events, feelings, and situations that are going on in your life. Writing about things that you feel grateful for may have multiple benefits: you may feel more positive about life, have fewer physical ailments, *and* find yourself working out more. You only need to do the gratitude exercise once a week, so it's a fairly impressive range of benefits for a pretty small investment of your time.

4

Making better decisions

'In all affairs it's a healthy thing now and then
to hang a question mark on the things you
have long taken for granted.'

Bertrand Russell

What sorts of decisions are you agonizing about in your life right now?

One of my clients initially came to me for advice because she was unsure about the direction her career should take. Eleanor, a 37-year-old lawyer, was wondering whether to quit a long-hours but highly paid job to work at a smaller law firm that would require fewer hours but also taking a substantial pay cut.

However, her situation turned out to be more complex than she originally let on. She was also trying to decide whether she should try to have a baby. She had never wanted to start a family in her 20s or early 30s. But now that she was getting older, she was afraid that not having a child might be a decision she would regret forever.

To make matters even more complicated, she was no longer sure that she wanted to stay with her long-term partner, Alex. He was a reliable partner but she was increasingly beginning to see his stability as cloying and dull.

Should she change jobs? Did she really want a baby at all? And if so, did she want to start a family with Alex? Or were some or all of these questions merely symptoms of something else that was troubling her?

Or consider the decisions facing other clients and friends of mine, too. Jason is pondering: should he and his wife sell their small house in bustling central London and move to a larger house in a quiet town in the country? Isabella is worrying whether to quit the family business in order to do something that may be more fulfilling but possibly more risky, too. Emma is wondering: should she buy a puppy or rescue an older dog? Keith has been told that his cancer has spread and is sadly wrestling over what to do next: should he attempt a fourth round of uncomfortable and emotionally draining chemotherapy or should he pursue one of the alternatives, none of which comes with a guarantee? Recruitment consultant Lawrence is contemplating whether to take a year-long sabbatical to travel and train as a yoga instructor.

When making such decisions, a major difficulty is that there is rarely a single 'right' or 'best' choice. It can feel confusing, scary, and worrying to weigh up all of the options on offer. But we're in luck. Groups of psychologists, mathematicians, and economists have been testing methods that can help to make such choices less agonizing. And in this chapter we'll look at a handful of the very best techniques that may help us to make better decisions.

Shaping the way you think

I'd like to begin by asking you to try a small challenge. I'll explain how it's relevant to making better decisions shortly. The challenge involves looking at 10 sets of words. Each set is made up of four words. And your task is to turn each set of words into a grammatical four-word sentence. It shouldn't take you very long at all.

has many patterns nature	employees must methodical be
ways in work systematic	precisely time measure clocks
shelves her Jennifer organized	efficient two-handed is typing
an form queue orderly	analytical investors be must
predictable times sunrise are	logic crimes requires solving

If you need the answers, you'll find them in the Notes at the back of the book.[1] But if you actually took the time to unscramble all 10 of the sentences, you are now – believe it or not – more likely to make better decisions.

The word unscrambling task works because it reminds you of the notion of structure and associated concepts, such as patterns, order, predictability, and causal relationships. And simply reminding yourself of the idea of structure in life may help you to make better decisions.

Across a series of studies, a team of research collaborators led by the University of Cincinnati's Ryan Rahinel showed that merely reminding people of the concept of structure helped them to make better decisions. For example, participants who unscrambled sentences that included words such as 'patterns' and 'organized' were more diligent in making their decisions than participants who unscrambled the same sentences except with words such as 'chance' and 'unpredictably'.

If you look back at the 10 scrambled sentences that I presented you, you'll see words such as 'efficient', 'logic', 'orderly', and 'precisely'. So you may have spotted the common theme connecting the sentences together.

But the work of Rahinel and his fellow investigators went on to show that even *incidental* reminders about the notion of structure could have a similar benefit. In a further study, the same team of researchers asked 92 participants to read an article about the growth of trees. Half of the participants read an article that described trees as growing in a way that created patterns and symmetry. The other half read a similar article, but this time describing trees as growing in a random and unsystematic fashion.

When the participants were then presented with a decision to be made, a clear difference again became apparent.

Participants who had read about the structured nature of tree growth spent longer on their decisions *and* afterwards said that they felt more certain they had made the right decisions.[2]

In writing up the results of their series of experiments, Rahinel and his colleagues suggested that the notion of structure – or the lack of it – may affect people without their knowledge. For example, simply living or working in an untidy, chaotic, unstructured environment may hamper people's decision-making. Yes, your home and work spaces may subtly but measurably impact your ability to make better decisions.

> Simply living or working in an untidy, chaotic, unstructured environment may hamper people's decision-making.

On a personal note, writing about this research finding had an immediate effect on my behaviour. I spent two minutes tidying my office desk!

Configuring your environment

The notion of structure increases the effort that people put into their decisions; it helps people to feel more confident – less emotionally ambivalent – about their ultimate choices, too. And the work of Ryan Rahinel and his collaborators suggests that both your physical *and* mental environments can affect your decision-making.

In terms of your physical environment, this research suggests that you may want to organize your work and home spaces. I don't want to get prescriptive about how much decluttering, tidying, and sorting out you should be doing. But if you do suspect that your work and living spaces are less than entirely helpful, then now may be the time to rethink them.

In terms of your mental environment, you could try this exercise which I have suggested to clients. Take around five minutes to write a few paragraphs about how you structured or organized a past project or assignment. It could be something in your work or home life, a major undertaking or a minor task. Simply write about what you did and how you imposed a plan or otherwise controlled or arranged things.

Once you've done that, you will have reminded yourself of the notion of structure. So then you should be better equipped to weigh up whatever issues or decisions you're facing.

Choosing the right decision-making strategy

My current smartphone is operating a little sluggishly, so I'm in the process of choosing a new one. The problem: there are so many to choose from. Should I go for Samsung, Apple, Google, Sony, Xiaomi, OnePlus, or another manufacturer? Then each phone differs in terms of price, screen size, screen resolution, weight, battery life, processor power, sound quality – the list goes on and on.

Now, an economist might suggest that the best way to choose a phone would be to draw up a definitive list of features associated with every phone on the market. Perhaps I could assign a score – say from 1 to 10 – for each phone attribute. For example, I might decide that one phone's camera deserves a mediocre 5 out of 10, while another phone's camera deserves a whopping 9 out of 10. And then I could add up all of the scores for each phone to come to a rational decision about the best phone for me.

Obviously, it would be massively time-consuming to evaluate the many dozens of phones out there in such a precise manner.

So an alternative decision-making strategy would be to look at a smaller number of phones and just a handful of the features that I find most relevant. For example, I don't want a phone that's too heavy – and it can't be so big that it can't fit into my trouser pocket. But I do want a good quality camera and lots of storage for the videos and photos I like to shoot. So maybe I could just focus on four factors: weight, size, camera quality, and storage. And I don't have the time to assess every single phone out there, so maybe I'll just have a look online at the top 15 or 20 phones available at the moment and choose one that way.

Psychologists led by Barry Schwartz from Swarthmore College distinguish between the two decision-making strategies. So taking a comprehensive approach in order to find the optimal choice is called maximizing. In contrast, finding something that's 'good enough' is called satisficing.[3]

> Finding something that's 'good enough'
> is called satisficing.

In theory, maximizing – spending lots of time and effort exploring every option – should lead to better choices. But that's not what the research shows. For example, consider a famous field experiment run by psychological scientists Sheena Iyengar from Columbia University and Mark Lepper from Stanford University. The research duo set up a tasting booth inside a gourmet supermarket in California offering shoppers the chance to peruse and buy a range of exotic jams. Sometimes, the booth offered shoppers an extensive array of 24 jams to choose from. At other times, the booth offered shoppers a much more limited choice of only six jams.

Now, you may imagine that shoppers were happier to be presented with the wider selection. Indeed, 60% of shoppers who saw the 24 jams stopped at the table to have a closer look. In contrast, only 40% of shoppers who were presented with the six-jam display stopped to look at them.

However, stopping to browse isn't really making a choice. And it was only when the researchers calculated how many people actually made a purchase that they spotted a clear difference. When presented with 24 different jams, a meagre 3% of shoppers (four people) ended up buying a jam. When presented with the much smaller display of only six jams, a massive 30% of the shoppers (31 people) made a purchase.[4]

That's a somewhat surprising result. Our instincts tell us that having more choice should make it easier for us to find something that perfectly meets our needs. But the opposite happens instead: having more options actually bewilders and overwhelms us – it makes it harder for us to make any decision at all.

> Having more options actually bewilders and overwhelms us – it makes it harder for us to make any decision at all.

The same result has been found in many areas of our lives. For instance, another study published in top science journal *Psychological Science* looked at the job hunting strategies used by graduating students who were looking for their first jobs out of university. The researchers – again led by Columbia University's Sheena Iyengar – asked 548 young men and women to describe their decision-making strategies in life.

Some of these participants were classified as maximizers – they strongly agreed with statements such as, 'I never settle for second best' and, 'Whenever I'm faced with a choice, I try to imagine what all the other possibilities are, even ones that aren't present at the moment'; these people generally wanted to look at as many alternatives as possible in order to find the best option. Others were classified as satisficers – they wanted to save time and effort by only looking at possibilities until they found something that they deemed good enough. For example, the maximizers said that they anticipated applying for an average of 20 jobs. In contrast, the satisficers anticipated that they would probably need to apply for only around 10 jobs.

Cutting a long story short, the satisficers actually ended up much happier with the outcomes of their job searches. The maximizers reported feeling more pessimistic, tired, anxious, stressed, worried, overwhelmed, and even depressed throughout the job hunting process.[5]

That's a whole big list of downsides associated with being a maximizer. So taking these sorts of studies into consideration, we know that people who use the maximizing strategy tend to be less happy with their choices in the end. One reason for this is that having to assess lots of options takes a great deal of brain power, so it's effortful and mentally exhausting. Humans are not robots who are able to make millions of calculations every second. The more alternatives you try to consider at once, the more you may come to realize that it's pretty much impossible to consider absolutely everything. And when – or if – you manage to make a decision, you may actually end up more worried about the trade-offs you made along the way and opportunities you may have missed.

> People who use the maximizing strategy tend to be less happy with their choices in the end.

In most arenas of life, it's simply not possible to make perfect decisions. When it comes to finding a job, there are probably hundreds – if not thousands – of other jobs that you could be doing. The same is true for your home, too: there are many other places where you could be living and, yes, several of them could be cheaper, cosier, or closer to the park. And what about if you're dating? Consider all of the singletons in your part of the world and there may well be someone out there who is kinder, funnier, tidier, more attractive, or adventurous, and so on. But are you really willing to date 10,000 people to find that so-called perfect person?

It may seem logical to try to maximize our search strategies for the perfect job, home, partner in life – or restaurant to visit, TV show to watch, or even book to read. But all that time spent anxiously weighing up options and feeling paralysed by choice may actually be better spent enjoying ourselves instead.

Learning to accept 'good enough' rather than chasing perfection

When it comes to making decisions, consider that the human brain is not really equipped to make so-called perfect decisions. When you're faced with a decision, accept that most people are actually happier finding something that's 'good enough' or even 'great' than when they spend overly long trying to find something that is the supposedly 'best' that it could possibly be.

By all means allow yourself an appropriate amount of time to collect information and weigh up alternatives. Choosing a car, a new laptop, a pension plan, or a new job isn't something that you should do in just a few minutes. But if you suspect that you're someone with perfectionistic tendencies, then ask friends and colleagues to help you to keep these instincts in check. Ask them occasionally: 'Have I got enough information to make a decision – or am I overthinking things and being indecisive now?'

Coping with information overload

Modern life offers us so many choices. And that choice can be overwhelming not just when buying a mobile phone, laptop, or other gadget or piece of technology. Imagine for a moment that you need to choose a pension provider. It's an important decision: picking a company that you hope will manage your money well enough so that you can have a happy, prosperous retirement. But again, the range of options can be perplexing.

Look online and you will find dozens and dozens of providers. Plus there are plenty of articles written by different journalists and supposed experts listing the 'top 10 private pensions' or the '12 best pension providers this year' – and such lists can sometimes recommend almost entirely different firms!

So how can you make a decision when you're faced with a lot of choice and you're far from being an expert on the topic?

This very problem was recently tackled in a journal called the *Review of Economics and Statistics*, which I'm sure is a gripping, page-turning read. Who needs Stephen King or James Patterson, right?

Anyway, a team of decision experts led by Tibor Besedes, a professor at Georgia Institute of Technology, ran an experiment asking two groups of participants to evaluate 16 complex healthcare packages. In order to incentivize the participants to concentrate and do their best, the researchers offered small cash prizes of up to $25 to participants who made what the experts judged to be better decisions.

The first group were allowed to mull over all 16 options at once. In other words, they used what's known as a simultaneous decision method in order to try to identify the best package overall.

That's like having glossy brochures for all 16 alternatives laid out on a table or all of the data in just the one spreadsheet at the same time.

Participants in the second group were asked to use what's known as the sequential tournament method: they were instructed to evaluate the 16 healthcare packages by looking at smaller groups of only four at a time.

So perhaps someone compared four companies named Ace, Best, Care, and Diamond to begin with. Once they had chosen the best package – the group winner – out of that group of four, they were asked to move on to the next group of maybe Extra, Finest, Glow, and Happy. Then Ignite, Jubilation, Kindred, and Lion. A fourth group might then have comprised Mighty, Nexus, Oasis, and Power.

Finally, the participants were told to compare the four group winners against each other – in our example that might have been Ace, Glow, Jubilation, and Mighty. In this final round, an ultimate, overall winner should emerge – perhaps that's Glow, for instance.

Anyway, I'm sure you get the idea. Rather than comparing all 16 options at once, these participants worked through five rounds of comparison in which there were only four options each time.

When Besedes and his colleagues analysed the results, they found that the sequential tournament method produced significantly better decisions. In fact, participants were roughly 50% more likely to identify what experts regarded as the best choice.

Of course, a 50% better chance of getting it right is a pretty big boost. However, when the researchers told the participants about the different methods and asked them which method they intended to use, they were surprised to find that the sequential tournament method was their least preferred option. In other words, it got the best result – but people were least inclined to use it.[6]

So here's the lesson. When it comes to making a decision amongst lots of choices, *don't* follow your gut. Our instinct is to compare all of the options against each other at once. However, research by behavioural economists suggests that we could help ourselves to make better decisions by using the sequential tournament method instead.

> We could help ourselves to make better decisions by using the sequential tournament method.

Using the sequential tournament method to make better decisions

Whenever you're facing an important decision that involves comparing a dozen or more options, consider using the sequential tournament method. You boost your chances of getting the best result by around 50%. Work through the following steps:

1. Divide however many options you have into groups of four (or so). For example, if you have 20 choices, that implies creating five groups of four. If you have 22 choices, that would mean you actually have several groups of four but two groups with five options in each.

2. Evaluate all of the options within each group and choose whichever you like best.

3. Put all of the individual group winners into a new winners group.

4. Finally, compare the individual round winners to decide on your best option.

The researchers found that the sequential tournament method worked for a wide variety of people – men and women of all ages and differing levels of education, too. But I think it's particularly relevant to those among us who are maximizers. So if you realize that you have somewhat perfectionistic, worrisome tendencies, then this method could help you to not only save time but also make better decisions, too. The way I think about it is that the sequential tournament method is about reducing the amount of information to be considered at any one time.

> The sequential tournament method is about reducing the amount of information to be considered at any one time.

Shall we work through an example together? Suppose I'm thinking about buying a used car, a hatchback with no more than 15,000 miles on it. I've decided that it has to have four-wheel drive and must be red. I also want to spend no more than £30,000.

I typed exactly this requirement into a popular car buying website and found 13 results. Using the sequential tournament method, I take the first four results and compare them against each other. So my first group consists of a Mercedes–Benz A45, an Audi A1, a Nissan Qashqai, and a Skoda Superb hatchback. Say I discount a few of them because I don't like the shades of red or for other reasons, and I decide that my favourite out of these four – the first group winner – is the Nissan Qashqai.

Then I look at the next group of four, which comprises a Mini Countryman Cooper, a Subaru XV, a Ford Edge, and a Volkswagen T-Roc. In this group, I like the Mini Countryman Cooper best.

Remember I have 13 options to compare in total. So my third group actually comprises five cars. And from this final group, I choose a Mitsubishi Eclipse Cross.

That leaves me to do one final round of comparisons between the Nissan Qashqai, the Mini Countryman Cooper, and the Mitsubishi Eclipse Cross. Which one wins? Of course it doesn't matter – it's just a hypothetical example. But here's the point: even though some part of my psyche may be telling me that I should just sit and compare all of my options at once, I should trust the science that this structured method will probably help me to make a better decision in the end.

Removing yourself from your situation

A 33-year-old friend of mine called Jerome recently started seeing a woman called Marla. There was a strong physical attraction between them and they spent a lot of time laughing together, too.

But after only six weeks together, Marla dropped a bombshell. Her application to transfer to an overseas branch of the bank she worked for had been accepted. In a few months, she would be taking on a new and exciting job – in Singapore. And she would likely be there for at least a year.

Jerome really liked Marla. He could imagine having a properly meaningful relationship with her. But she was due to move nearly 7,000 miles and eight time zones around the world. So should he continue to date her, probably develop deeper feelings for her – and risk possible later heartbreak? Or should he break off the promising new relationship in order to avoid getting more emotionally involved?

Jerome really couldn't make up his mind what to do so, over coffees, I suggested that he should take himself out of the picture. I asked him to imagine that it was a friend of his who was facing a similar situation.

'How would you advise this friend?' I asked Jerome.

A few days later, he messaged me to say that he had broken off the nascent relationship. When he had imagined how to counsel someone else, he had decided that they probably wouldn't have enough time in only a few months to cement the relationship sufficiently for it to survive being long-distance.

Less than a week later, Jerome was certain that he had made the right decision. And he was already exchanging messages with other potential dates.

Of course, the idea of thinking through a difficult decision by imagining it's happening to someone else is backed by science. Igor Grossman, a behavioural scientist at the University of Waterloo in Canada, is perhaps the leader in this field of research. In multiple studies, he and his colleagues have found that people make better – or what he and his research collaborators call *wiser* – decisions when taught to adopt a 'self-distanced', third-person perspective.[7]

> People make better decisions when taught to adopt a 'self-distanced', third-person perspective.

For example, suppose that I (the author, Rob Yeung) have been offered a book deal by a publishing company. However, they want me to complete the 60,000-word manuscript in only three months' time. To help me to make the best decision, I might write down benefits of the book deal such as, 'Rob would earn a good fee from writing this book' and, 'He would get his name out to a new audience of readers' but also downsides such as, 'Rob would probably get really grouchy and tired from having to do three hours of research and writing every weeknight.'

So one way of using the technique is to use your own name and to consider what he or she should do. But an alternative thought exercise could also prove useful.

More intriguingly, University of Minnesota researchers have found benefits from imagining how a fictional character might handle the same situation. Investigators Rachel White and Stephanie Carlson asked children as young as 3 years of age to solve a series of problems under different conditions. Some of the children were told to adopt a first-person perspective: to use the pronoun 'I' when solving the puzzles. A second group were instructed to take on the self-distanced perspective by talking to themselves using their own names. But a third group were asked to pretend that they were somebody else entirely and given four choices of character: Batman, Bob the Builder, Dora the Explorer, and Rapunzel.

After testing nearly a hundred children, the researchers found that 3-year-olds were too young to benefit from the techniques. However, 5-year-olds did perform better when they adopted the self-distanced, third-person perspective as opposed to the first-person perspective. They also did better when they took on the identity of a fictional character.[8]

Of course, that study was conducted with very young children. But other studies confirm that adults who imagine that a problem is affecting someone other than themselves also solve problems more effectively.[9] And that sort of makes sense. After all, there are plenty of adults who ask themselves: 'What would Jesus do?' And I've heard people asking themselves: 'What would Beyoncé do?' too.

Taking a step back from what's going on around you

Adopting a different point of view – specifically, the self-distanced, third-person perspective – enables better decisions and judgements. This technique has been proven in not only personal decision-making but also when participants have been asked to assess tricky social, economic, or political issues – such as funding cuts in education or the impact of climate change.[10]

The next time you are torn between options or trying to evaluate how best to deal with a difficult situation, imagine that you are advising someone else. Perhaps put pen to paper to write down what this person who happens to share your name is thinking and feeling. You could use your own name to write about what this person is thinking or feeling. Or simply use third-person pronouns to talk about what 'he' is thinking and feeling or what 'she' could do next.

Plenty of other studies have shown that writing in the third-person also helps people to feel less emotional. So perhaps pretending to advise someone else works because it allows us to distance ourselves from our anger, fear, sadness, and other feelings and therefore make decisions that are more rational.

The next time you are trying to evaluate how best to deal with a difficult situation, imagine that you are advising someone else.

Onwards and upwards

- Consider that incidental – seemingly irrelevant – reminders about the idea of structure may help you to make better decisions. So consider the amount of structure in both your physical *and* mental environments. In the physical world, even having a tidier room and a more organized desk could help you to make more confident decisions. Or to prepare yourself mentally, write about a time you structured or organized either an assignment at work or a project in your home life.

- Remember the differences between the maximizing versus satisficing styles of decision-making. Maximizing may in theory seem a better bet, but remember that we humans have only limited information-processing capabilities. Satisficing is about investing enough time to find something that's 'good' or even 'great' as opposed to wearing yourself out by trying to find that elusive 'perfect' something that may not actually exist. If you have perfectionistic, indecisive tendencies, ask your friends, 'Am I overthinking this?'

- When faced with choice overload – for example when you have a dozen or more choices – use the sequential tournament method to reduce the strain on your brain. Divide up however many options you have into groups of around four. Choose the best option from each of those groups. Then do a final comparison of those best options to select your ultimate choice.

- When faced with just about any other kind of difficult decision, imagine how you would advise a friend in an identical situation. Write using different pronouns – talk about what 'he' or 'she' should do and 'his' or 'her' options. Or use your own name to self-distance from the problem and allow you better clarity of thought.

5

Boosting your creativity and inventiveness

'Imagination is more important than knowledge.'

Albert Einstein

What does the word 'creativity' mean to you? If you're like most people, you have probably never given it much thought. Or perhaps you think of it as a skill or quality that people only need if they're involved in painting, film making, fashion, or the arts. But I'd argue that it's one of the most important skills to develop if you want to improve your career, health, relationships, finances, or just about any other part of your life.

Because I and other psychologists think of creativity as the process of improving things, saving time, saving money, and doing things better than before. And who doesn't want to be able to improve things, save time, and do things better?

Perhaps you're looking for a way to repair something around the house and you don't have quite the right tools or materials – you'll have to find some other way of doing it. Or you're studying and want to figure out a better system for organizing your notes so that you can revise more effectively. Maybe you're trying to motivate a colleague, surprise a friend, or inject a spark into your relationship. You're a parent looking for a way to keep the kids entertained. Or you're an executive trying to come up with a product or service that your customers will want to buy. All of these situations would benefit from an idea or two – and of course that requires creativity.

Now, there are some people who believe that creativity is a gift, something innate that you're born with – that you've either got or not. But that's not what the research seems to indicate. Dozens of studies confirm that creativity is not fixed – it is affected by how you think, how you feel, and what's going on around you at any moment in time. In other words, you can consciously choose to expand your horizons and become more creative whenever you're ready to do so.

> Studies confirm that creativity is not fixed – it is affected by how you think, how you feel, and what's going on around you.

Allowing yourself to deserve greater creativity

Before we look at how to boost your creativity, allow me to ask you a question. Exactly how creative do you think you are?

Research psychologists test people's creativity in a variety of ways. To illustrate one such method, suppose for a moment that you've volunteered for a study on creativity. You arrive at the experimenter's laboratory and you're told that you're going to be given a short test of your ability to generate ideas.

The researcher asks you to sit down. She gives you a pen and sheets of paper and says: 'I'd like you to imagine that a restaurant has recently closed down and vacated a space. The restaurant has removed all of the fittings and fixtures, so the space is now completely empty. I'd like you to spend five minutes coming up with as many ideas as you can for how you could fill the space.'

She checks that you understand the task. And then she clicks a stopwatch to give you exactly five minutes for the task.

Once your time is up, she would take your responses away to be evaluated by at least two experts, who would rate the creativity of your ideas.

This idea generation test is widely used to measure the kind of creativity that helps people to come up with practical yet novel solutions – what's called 'divergent creativity' by psychologists.

And to keep things fresh, researchers often change the situation. For example, they could ask you to come up with as many uses of a spoon as possible. Or as many ways as you can identify for reducing pollution and protecting the environment.

Anyway, researchers Emily Zitek from Cornell University and Lynne Vincent from Vanderbilt University in Nashville found that participants' idea generation was significantly boosted by a five-minute writing exercise. Actually, the researchers found that the writing exercise enhanced creativity on several other tests of creative thinking, too, including a drawing task in which people had to use their imagination to sketch things they had never seen before.

So what did this writing exercise involve?

The researchers asked experimental participants to write about why they should demand the best in life, why they deserved more than others, and why they should get their way in life. In other words, the participants were asked to think about why they might be better than others and worthy of good things.

Other groups of control participants wrote about why they should *not* demand the best in life, why they did *not* deserve more than others, and why they should *not* expect to get their own way in life. When the creative outputs of the two writing exercises were compared, it became clear that the experimental participants who boosted their own self-worth performed significantly more creatively. For example, when asked to come up with creative ideas for possible uses of a paperclip, the experimental participants not only came up with more ideas in total – their responses were judged by experts to have been more genuinely novel, too.[1] In other words, the self-worth writing exercise boosted not only the quantity but also the quality of ideas.

Clearly, no one would ever deliberately write about why they should not demand the best, why they do not deserve more than others, and why they should not expect to get their way in life. But the unfortunate truth is that it's easy sometimes to feel defeated and down or to repeat negative messages to ourselves, such as, 'I'm no good' or, 'I'll never get what I want.' Especially when we've experienced rejection or failure, we may inadvertently lower our own expectations.

> The unfortunate truth is that it's easy sometimes to feel defeated and down or to repeat negative messages to ourselves.

I work with many clients who come to me because they feel down or stuck in a rut. Many feel chronically overlooked at work or have suffered setbacks in their personal lives. Others have been rejected repeatedly by employers. Unfortunately, that can put them into a vicious cycle. Their knockbacks make them feel depressed and disappointed. And that disappointment makes them less creative and less able to find novel solutions that would help them to escape their situations.

This self-worth technique may work because it breaks that cycle. Reminding ourselves that we are worthy seems to boost creativity because it helps us to see that we are different. When we feel more unique and special, we become more willing to challenge conventions and break rules, which results in more legitimately creative thinking.

So, the next time you want to come up with a breakthrough idea or a novel solution to a problem, consider prepping yourself mentally first. Remind yourself why you should expect to achieve your goals in life and you may help yourself to unlock your creative talents.

Feeling that you're worthy of creativity

Based on the instructions used by researchers Emily Zitek and Lynne Vincent, you should be able to boost your divergent creativity by spending a few minutes writing out your responses to three questions. For each question, you need to come up with three answers.

● Why should you demand the best in life?

● Why do you deserve more than other people?

● Why should you get your way in life?

Remember that you need to list three reasons for each of the three questions. So that means you need to come up with nine responses in total. Once you've spent a few minutes coming up with your nine reasons, you should be better mentally equipped to think more creatively.

> When we feel more unique and special,
> we become more willing to challenge conventions
> and break rules.

Allowing yourself to step back in time

Back in the late-1990s, I started my career as a strategic management consultant for a large American consulting firm, where I mainly spent time analysing costs and sales figures to help clients identify new ways of making more money. And I would often hear from clients and colleagues that they wanted more creative solutions – that they wanted to 'think outside of the box' or engage in 'blue-sky thinking'. I even remember one client saying that we should think 'as if there is no box'.

This kind of talk has largely fallen out of fashion. In fact, if you use these phrases nowadays, you're more likely to elicit sniggers of derision or eye rolls behind your back. But the message behind such sayings is that creative thinking often involves breaking the rules, going against the status quo, ignoring what everyone else seems to be doing, and imagining that anything is possible.

The thing is, we all used to be much better at thinking truly creatively than we are now. Turn back the clock to when we were young children and of course we didn't know what the rules were. We weren't aware of there being a status quo. We made up monsters and aliens, fairies and imaginary settings – and we did whatever we liked.

> Turn back the clock to when we were young children who didn't yet know what the rules were.

Growing up is about learning to behave in ways that society deems appropriate. Being a good team player in the workplace often requires that we follow the rules – both explicit rules as well as unspoken ones – about how things should or should not be done. We learn to stick to routines and not blurt out everything that we think. Ultimately, we learn that we as adults shouldn't be silly or foolish – it's a slur for someone to say that another adult is *childish*. But, being childish on occasion may actually help us to be more creative.

Research backs up our intuitions that kids really are less bound by rules. In the 1980s, for example, researchers Elizabeth Rosenblatt and Ellen Winner spent time analysing the drawings created by children of various ages and concluded that children tended to fall into three distinct phases of creative thinking, which they termed the preconventional, conventional, and postconventional years.

Preconventional children younger than around 8 years of age created pieces of art that often seemed weird, wrong, or incomplete. For instance, a picture of 'my dad' might have had too many arms or too miniscule a head. But Rosenblatt and Winner found that these children tended to produce the most truly original art – not dissimilar from the fantastical, abstract creations of Pablo Picasso or Paul Klee. These kids hadn't learnt the conventions about what drawings should or shouldn't look like.

Children aged around 8 to 12 years fell into the conventional category: their art tended to be increasingly guided by conventions about how pictures should look. And children aged from 12 years onwards were considered postconventional, as most of them by now had learnt to respect the customary ways of depicting people, animals, objects, and scenes.[2]

OK. So young kids may genuinely be more creative. But how does that help us adults?

> Simply encouraging adults to adopt a more childlike state of mind could help to boost creativity.

Psychological investigators Darya Zabelina and Michael Robinson from North Dakota State University wondered if simply encouraging adults to adopt a more childlike state of mind could help to boost creativity. They recruited 76 undergraduate students into an experiment and asked them all to take a series of tests of divergent creative thinking.

Just prior to taking the tests, though, the students were asked to spend just seven minutes writing a short essay. They were instructed to imagine that classes had been cancelled and that they had the whole day free for themselves. The students were then asked to write what they would do with their time.

But there was a small twist to the experiment. Half of the students read a set of instructions with just five extra words in it. They were told: 'You are 7 years old.'

Students in the study who imagined they had the day off as adults tended to write how they would check their emails, catch up on sleep, do chores, go to the gym, and catch up on their studies. But here's an example of what one student wrote when instructed to imagine being 7 years old again:

> I would start off by going to the ice-cream shop and getting the biggest cone I could get. I would then go to the pet store and look at all the dogs. After that I would go visit my grandma and play a few games of gin. Then she would make me cookies and give me a huge glass of milk. I would then go for a walk, where I would meet up with my friends and we would play in the park…

Clearly, the researchers expected that imagining themselves as 7-year-olds would boost the students' creativity. But what would the benefits be exactly?

Well, it turned out that the two groups came up with the same numbers of ideas. The students who had written about themselves as 7-year-olds came up with no more ideas than the students who had written about their adult days off.

The difference between the two groups only became apparent when the originality of the various ideas was assessed by external experts. Writing as 7-year-olds helped those participants to generate ideas that were judged as more original and unique.[3]

In other words, taking themselves back to their childhoods had not helped them to create *more* ideas. But it did help them to come up with *better*, more intriguingly novel ideas. Or, to put it in still another way, adopting a childlike mindset seems to affect the quality rather than the quantity of ideas.

Stripping away adult assumptions and conventions

The researchers Darya Zabelina and Michael Robinson point out that growing up and maturing into adulthood typically leads to ways of thinking and behaving that are 'more rule bound, more routine, and often less flexible and creative'. However, their research suggests that simply writing about a situation as if you were a 7-year-old child can at least temporarily help you to step free of some of these rules and conventions.

If you wish to boost the originality of your thinking, first allow yourself between 5 and 10 minutes to write about a day's activities as if you were a 7-year-old child. Draw upon your memories of favourite activities and use your imagination to describe how you might spend your time. No one else will see what you write, so really go for it in allowing yourself to be genuinely playful, curious, and childish.

Perhaps you are worried about coming across as silly or foolish by pretending you're a 7-year-old. There may be other adults – your boss, colleagues, friends, or family – who will sneer at such a notion. But no one says that you have to tell people that's what you're doing. This can be a secret technique between just me and you. Just remember that writing as if you're a child is a preparatory exercise that will get you geared up to be more creative. But you still then have to spend some time actually trying to be more creative.

Anyway, trust the research. If you want to improve your divergent creativity and come up with more genuinely different ideas, encourage yourself to recapture the spirit of play and unfettered exploration that are so characteristic of young children. And reap the benefits of more childlike – in a good way – thinking.

> To come up with more genuinely different ideas, encourage yourself to recapture the spirit of play and unfettered exploration that are so characteristic of young children.

Harnessing the creative psychology of sound

Have you noticed that there seem to be more and more coffee shops springing up? Personally, I'm rather pleased that there are growing numbers of independent coffee shops offering better quality coffee than the big chains can offer. They also provide pleasant environments in which to work – I do a lot of my research reading while out and about rather than at my desk or at home.

Clearly, I'm not the only one who likes working in them, either. Walk into most coffee shops and you'll often see half of the patrons tapping away on laptops or on their phones. So why do so many people like working from these little venues? Could it be that something about coffee shops actually helps us to work better?

> Could it be that something about coffee shops actually helps us to work better?

These were the sorts of questions explored in a series of studies led by Ravi Mehta, a professor specializing in business and marketing at the University of Illinois at Urbana–Champaign. In particular, he and his research team set out to look at the effects of ambient (background) noise on creative output.

The researchers began by recording ambient noise from three locations: inside a cafeteria, next to a roadside, and in the vicinity of construction work. They then blended the sounds to create a single track of mixed background noise.

Next, Mehta and his colleagues played the background noise to groups of participants at different volumes. Some heard quiet background noise (measuring 50 decibels in volume), others moderate noise (70 decibels), and a third group loud noise (85 decibels). A fourth group sat in an otherwise quiet room.

Participants in all four groups then took a test of creativity called the remote associates test. You can try it if you like. Imagine being presented with rows of three words at a time. Your challenge is to think creatively in order to identify a fourth word that conceptually connects the first three, remotely associated, words.

For example, I might give you the following three words:

falling	dust	actor

A correct connecting word for that trio would be 'star'. We can talk about a 'falling star' and the cosmic particles known as 'stardust'. But notice that 'star' can also be a colloquial word for an actor – so the connecting word only has to *relate* to all of the first three words. You don't necessarily have to use the connecting word to create further words or phrases.

Have a go at a handful – I'll pop the answers in the Notes at the end of the book:[4]

skate	water	cream
wheel	high	rocking
out	dog	home
lock	line	end
female	flower	friend

Hopefully, you can see that the remote associates test requires a form of lateral thinking. You have to be able to summon up a way to connect concepts that at first may seem unrelated.

It's a kind of creative proficiency that could be useful in all sorts of real-life contexts. For example, you may get home late from work one evening to find you only have three items in your fridge. How can you boil, bake, grill, or otherwise combine them to produce an edible dinner? Or suppose your company is known for manufacturing a limited number of products and now you want to launch a service that complements your original product line.

Anyway, back to the experimental investigation. The researchers found that 70 decibels of noise boosted creativity as compared with 85 decibels, 50 decibels, or no additional background noise.

But unless you're a physicist or sound engineer, allow me to put those numbers into context. Eighty-five decibels is loud. It's the sound of an extremely loud alarm clock. Or perhaps the level of noise you'd be exposed to if you were standing in the middle of several lanes of fast-moving traffic. In fact, the Health and Safety Executive in the UK mandates that employers must provide hearing protection for workers who are constantly exposed to sound at this level.

Fifty decibels is a level of background noise that most people may not even notice. Sit in your kitchen and the compressor of your refrigerator is probably generating a hum at around 50 decibels. Or it's the level of noise that you may hear if you're caught in a light rain shower.

In contrast, 70 decibels is typical of a bustling – but not overly frantic – restaurant or coffee shop. With this level of background noise, you may have to raise your voice slightly to be heard.

So 70 decibels was the optimum level for creativity as measured by the remote associates test. And this level of noise was found to be best again and again when the research team measured creativity using several other tests of creativity across a series of five experiments in total.[5]

> People are generally more creative when they're exposed to moderate amounts of noise.

People are generally more creative when they're exposed to moderate amounts of noise. But why? Well, creativity can't be forced. The brain needs to be able to dream and drift and jump from one thought to the next. And Mehta and his fellow investigators found that ambient noise 'induces processing disfluency'.

In plain English, noise is distracting. And being a little distracted by a moderate (70 decibel) level of noise seems to allow our brains to freewheel and think more laterally. But too much noise (at the 85 decibel level) is so distracting that it actually disrupts our ability to think at all – let alone creatively.

Finding your sonic sweet spot

Research by Ravi Mehta and his colleagues found that a background level of noise of 70 decibels helped experimental participants to be more creative than those exposed to either 50 or 85 decibels of noise.

I'm not arguing that you should buy a sound meter to measure the ambient noise around you at any moment in time. However, the research suggests that it might be an idea to be more aware of what's going on around you and find ways to shape your environment to fit your creative needs.

If you work in a very noisy environment, consider heading to your cafeteria or a local coffee shop when you want to think more creatively. Or if that's not possible, consider wearing noise-cancelling headphones or even humble earplugs to bring things down to a more tolerable level.

On the other hand, if you work in a very quiet space – for example you work from home or in an isolated studio – also consider heading somewhere a bit more bustling. Or pop on headphones and install a white noise app on your phone. Many of these apps are free – and they may allow you to choose from a menu of sounds: wildlife, thunderstorms, coffee shops, passing traffic, and so on.

I'll finish this section with a couple of caveats, a few words of warning. First of all, the research does *not* say that being exposed to moderate levels of sound benefitted all aspects of work productivity. Seventy decibels only boosted creativity, that particular capacity that allows us to come up with novel ideas. So don't blast yourself with background noise expecting that it will definitely help you to work on a spreadsheet, learn material for an exam, write a report, or other tasks. Who knows? It may help. But as the relevant studies haven't been done yet, we just don't know either way.

Secondly, notice that I recommend background noise as opposed to background music. And that's because music may actually impair rather than enhance creativity. Researchers headed up by Emma Threadgold at the University of Central Lancashire recently played different types of music to participants while they tried to solve a variant of the remote associates test.

Some participants listened to instrumental music without lyrics; others listened to music with English lyrics; still others listened to music with foreign lyrics. Yet all three types of music actually reduced people's creativity.[6]

> Music may actually impair rather than
> enhance creativity.

So background noise may be good for creativity. But background music may not be.

Of course, you're free to do as you wish. But for these reasons, I'm listening to the sounds of rain and thunder through a Bluetooth speaker as I type these very words.

Allowing body and mind to wander

Not long ago, I worked with the creative director of an award-winning advertising agency in Soho, central London. The agency has created some of the most famous campaigns on the planet for well-known car manufacturers, makes of jeans, mobile phone companies, and other brands that you'd recognize.

The creative director, a grizzled, tanned man in his late 50s who dressed as fashionably as someone in his 20s, claimed that many of his best ideas came to him when he went for a walk around his office block. Earlier in his career, he used to go outside up to several dozen times a day in order to smoke a cigarette – and rather than just stand there smoking, he decided that he may as well take the opportunity to go for a brisk walk. He quit smoking around a decade ago, but he still goes for frequent walks.

He was adamant that his walks helped him to conceive some of his very best ideas. And he suggested that everybody should do the same. But the problem with such advice is that it is potentially too specific. That is to say, does going for a brisk walk only benefit creative directors who work in advertising? Or can it help everybody to be more creative?

> Simply going for a walk may boost divergent creativity.

Stanford University researchers Marily Oppezzo and Daniel Schwartz suspected that simply going for a walk may boost divergent creativity. But they tested it in a frankly ingenious fashion.

The enterprising researchers recruited 40 adults into an experiment testing their creativity. But the pair of investigators did not merely examine people's creativity after, say, just walking versus sitting. Before testing their creativity, the researchers actually split their participants into four groups, and asked each group to do a different activity.

One group sat indoors in the laboratory (which we shall call the sat-in condition). A second group walked on a treadmill inside the laboratory (walk-in).

A third group walked outdoors along a path that took them through the university's campus (walk-out). And the final group sat in wheelchairs and were pushed around by research assistants outdoors for the same length of time (sat-out).

Can you see what the researchers did? I think this was really clever, because the researchers were essentially able to test the effects of two separate conditions: walking (versus sitting) and being outdoors (versus being indoors).

The researchers sent all of the participants' creativity tests off to be scored by an expert who was not told of the different groups. And when the results came back, they found that the participants who had been seated in the laboratory (sat-in) generated on average 3.5 novel ideas.

In contrast, participants who walked on the treadmill (walk-in) generated 5.3 new ideas. So just going for a walk was clearly beneficial.

Furthermore, the group who sat in wheelchairs and were pushed around outdoors (sat-out) generated 4.9 novel ideas. These participants didn't get to exercise but still were significantly more creative than those who had sat indoors. Evidently, the act of being outdoors in itself also boosts creativity.

However, the participants who walked outdoors (walk-out) were the most creative of all, coming up with 9.3 new ideas on average. Contrasted with the 3.5 ideas generated by those who sat indoors, that's plainly a gigantic advantage.[7]

Spelling it out, it seems that there are two separate effects at play here. Going for a walk boosts creativity. Being outdoors also boosts creativity. But you get the biggest boost by combining the two and going for a walk outdoors.

Going for a walk boosts creativity. Being outdoors also boosts creativity.

So it turns out that the creative director at that advertising agency was right: getting outside for a walk might have been a big contributor to his creativity. But the research accords with my own experience, too.

For the years that I've been taking our family dog Byron for walks, I've frequently found many of my best ideas coming to me while strolling along pavements or wandering in parks. As a result, I always have my phone with me so that I can capture thoughts whenever they occur to me.

I often take Byron and my laptop with me to coffee shops, too. And it's often during these sessions that I have some of my best breakthroughs in terms of how to structure a book chapter or write up a particular piece of research. It all makes total sense now. When I first came across the science – not only on walking outdoors but also the study on ambient noise by Ravi Mehta and his colleagues – I could see that some of my solutions may have come about as a combination of three factors: walking, being outdoors, *and* being exposed to the hubbub of a bustling coffee shop.

Exercising your creativity

The study by Marily Oppezzo and Daniel Schwartz shows that both walking and being outdoors can separately benefit creativity. Go for a walk indoors and you should be able to get a measurable boost to your creativity, your ability to come up with novel ideas. So how about simply walking around your building for a while?

Or another way to improve your creativity is to get outdoors. Simply sitting outside may provide enough mental stimulation to enhance your creativity. However, for the biggest uplift to your creativity, combine the two activities and go for a walk outside.

Of course, walking doesn't just boost our creativity. We all know that walking is good for our bodies – it helps to keep us physically fit and healthy. But walking also has other psychological benefits. I actually gained my PhD, my doctorate in psychology, by investigating the psychological antecedents and consequences of exercise. Or, in non-jargon-laden English, why do only some people exercise – and what do they get out of it?

In one study, a colleague and I found that just 15 minutes of moderately challenging exercise elevated people's mood significantly more than the same period of time spent sitting and resting quietly.[8] But later research has shown that exercise doesn't even have to be moderately challenging: even walking for as little as 10 to 15 minutes can measurably improve people's mood, too.[9]

In Chapter 1, we discussed methods for beating stress. But walking really is a win–win–win technique that helps us to be better in all sorts of ways. We win because we burn calories and keep our bodies fit and healthy. We win because we lift our mood and keep stress at bay. And we win because we take our creativity to a higher level, too.

> Walking really is a win–win–win technique that helps us to be better in all sorts of ways.

Introducing mental constraints to boost creative thinking

So far in this chapter we have covered a wide variety of methods for enhancing creativity that have spanned applying psychological techniques, changing our physical environments, and putting our bodies into motion. But I'll finish by introducing a simple method that I frequently use when I'm running workshops with business owners or teams of managers who are trying to come up with genuinely novel thinking.

A group of Dutch researchers led by Eric Rietzschel from the University of Groningen in the Netherlands wanted to explore people's creativity under different circumstances. Are people more creative when given broad problems to solve? Or do people generate better ideas when their attention is focused on narrower, more specific problems?

For example, imagine that you're the owner of a small chain of clothing shops that sells to men, women, and children. You want your employees to come up with ideas on how to make the business more successful. A broad question might be something like: 'What ideas do you have for selling more clothes to customers?' In contrast, a narrower question might be: 'What ideas do you have for selling more women's clothes?'

Or say you run a school cafeteria and want ideas on how you could encourage the children you feed to eat more healthily. You could ask your colleagues a broad question such as: 'How could we persuade our school kids to make better food choices?' Or you could ask a more targeted question such as: 'How could we get our school kids to eat more vegetables?'

Anyway, Rietzschel and his colleagues asked 102 undergraduate psychology students to consider one of two questions. Half of the students were given a broad question: about how they could make possible improvements to do with 'the education at the department of psychology'. The other half were given a narrower question: how they could make improvements specifically to do with the 'lectures at the department of psychology'.

Of course, lectures are a narrower topic because they are just a subset of the overall educational experience, which involves essays, group work, exams, and other scholastic tools. But it's time to take a guess now. Would broad or narrow questions be better for boosting creativity?

When I first came across this conundrum, I reasoned that broad questions may lead to greater creativity. After all, a broad question means fewer constraints. So I supposed that it would lead to freer, crazier, more novel thinking.

But I was wrong. Because it turned out that narrower instructions in the experiment actually led to a greater number of more original ideas.

The researchers found that participants generated no more ideas in total when given the narrower instructions. However, there was a higher proportion of ideas that was judged to have been genuinely innovative. In other words, a narrow frame of reference (like most of the other techniques in this chapter) does not affect the quantity of ideas – it just elevates their quality.[10]

> A narrow frame of reference does not affect the quantity of ideas – it just elevates their quality.

Tackling problems and opportunities one at a time

If you want to generate more truly original ideas, consider carving up your overall issue into a number of smaller questions. Of course, this means that it may take longer to cover the whole issue, but try to see it as an investment that should ultimately result in better-quality ideas. For example, avoid asking the members of your family a broad question such as, 'How can we reduce household costs?' Instead, you could try focusing their attention on smaller, more manageable questions such as, 'How can we reduce our utility bills?' and, 'How can we reduce our grocery costs?'

Or if you're a business manager and want to boost customer service, a broad (and less effective) question might be, 'How could we improve customer service?' In contrast, narrower, more directed questions might include: 'How could we improve customer service to our top 50 customers?' and, 'How could we improve customer service in each of our geographical regions?'

Adopting a narrower frame may work because it pushes us off the path of least resistance. When we are allowed to generate ideas relating to a broad topic, our brains may choose the easiest options – to focus on the ideas that take the least effort to generate. In contrast, when we focus only on a particular aspect or subcategory of the overall problem, our brains may be forced to work harder. And that extra level of effort may help us to identify ideas that really are just that little bit more creative.

Onwards and upwards

- To boost your creativity, help yourself to feel special and unique first. Spend a few minutes writing about why you should demand the best in life, why you deserve more than other folks, and why you should get your way in life. Feeling this way every day is unlikely to be helpful in all aspects of real life – you could come across as a bit of a brat – but as a one-off exercise this has been shown to result in better creative thinking.

- In order to open your mind up to creative possibilities, set aside time to write about how you might spend a day if you were 7 years old again. Remember that this kind of exercise may seem frivolous or stupid to some people, but you don't ever have to show what you write to anyone else. You don't even have to tell people you use this kind of exercise.

- Be more aware of the amount of background noise that you're exposed to. Remember that very quiet environments may not always be the most conducive for creativity. At the same time, bear in mind that very noisy environments are also likely to reduce creativity.

- Remember that one of the most powerful interventions available to you is simply to go for a walk. Even walking around indoors boosts creativity (as well as mood). But for the largest benefit to your creative thinking, go for a walk outdoors – and of course you exercise your body and may end up in a better mood, too.

- To generate ideas that are significantly more novel, consider focusing on narrower issues. Recall that asking a broad question such as, 'How can I be happier at work?' tends to result in fewer truly original ideas than narrower questions such as, 'How can I be happier in my relationships with my teammates?' and, 'How can I be happier in my work with customers?' However, do keep in mind that you may need to allow more time to consider a number of narrower questions.

6

Being clever about learning, memory, and performance

'Minds are like parachutes. They only function when they are open.'

James Dewar

Learning isn't just something we need to do when we're at school. The world is constantly changing and we need to keep learning and getting better at what we do – or risk getting left behind. And I'm not just talking about changes in technology either. Health advice changes: eat more of this but definitely don't eat that. Politicians change. Businesses change. The things that society deems acceptable to say to each other – and the things we definitely should not say – change, too.

Maybe you need to commit to memory your company's latest products and services. Or you want to pick up some words and phrases in French, Spanish, or Mandarin Chinese in order to get by on an upcoming trip. Perhaps you want to learn a skill such as knitting or piano, ice skating or golf.

Learning is an ongoing, lifelong process. But I recently came across great news! I read on a website that scientists had managed to boost learning fairly significantly – just by getting experimental participants to skip the occasional meal.

Shouldn't be too difficult, right? And, given that around two-thirds of adults in many Western countries are overweight or even obese, perhaps that could be good for our waistlines, too.[1]

Unfortunately, it only became apparent in the second paragraph of the article that the experimental participants had not been human. They weren't even dogs or mice. They had been nematode roundworms.[2]

Now, I'm not saying that eating less does *not* boost learning and memory in humans. It may do. Or it may not. The point is that there is no conclusive evidence to say what the effect of occasional fasting may be. We just can't say yet.

Unfortunately, the study supposedly boosting learning – in nematode roundworms – isn't the only one. I often come across misleading headlines in the media claiming that doing X or Y can boost learning, skill acquisition, and memory retention. But dig deeper and you may discover that some methods have only been tested in non-human animals. Others aren't backed by evidence at all. So in this chapter, we'll run through four of the best techniques that have been proven to boost (human) learning, memory, and performance.

> The world is constantly changing and we need to keep learning and getting better at what we do – or risk getting left behind.

Reconstructing knowledge to enhance learning

When you have to study for a test or exam, how do you like to learn?

Over the years, I've come across all sorts of study methods. Some people like to use coloured pens to highlight important phrases in textbooks that they've bought. Others like to write out notes based on their textbooks. A few try to summarize their thoughts onto small note cards. Another option is to draw diagrams to try to represent the relationships among key concepts. A lot of people just read, read, and re-read their books and notes. But what actually works?

Psychological scientist Jeffrey Karpicke is a well-respected authority at Purdue University in the field of learning and memory research. In a now-famous study published in the top journal *Science*, Karpicke and his collaborator, Janell Blunt, set out to test a handful of common methods used by students and learners all over the world. They took 80 students and asked all of them to study a short text on the science of sea otters, a topic which was chosen for its relative obscurity. The students were then divided into four groups and given different instructions on how they should go about learning the materials for a later test:

- The first study group were given just five minutes to read and memorize as much as they could from the entire text.

- The second study group were given the chance to study the text several times. These participants studied for five minutes then had a one-minute break. They then studied for a further five minutes and had another one-minute break. They repeated this twice more until they had had a total study time of 20 minutes.

- The third group were given an initial five minutes to read the materials before being taught a learning method called concept mapping. A concept map is a diagram in which ideas are represented as nodes and the relationships between them are represented by lines. (As an example, I've included below just one quarter of the overall concept map for this book – this part summarizes the Introduction and first three chapters of the book.) These participants were given 25 minutes to refer to the text on sea otters and create a concept map based on what they took from it.

- The fourth group were given only five minutes to read the text. The text was then taken away and the poor participants were asked to take a surprise written test on what they had learnt. The test lasted 10 minutes. Then they were given a further five minutes to study the text before being subjected to yet another 10-minute test of their recall.

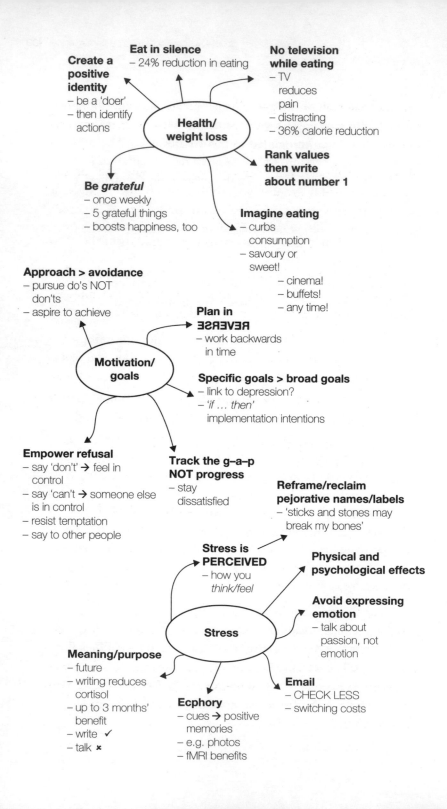

Create a positive identity
– be a 'doer'
– then identify actions

Eat in silence
– 24% reduction in eating

No television while eating
– TV reduces pain
– distracting
– 36% calorie reduction

Health/ weight loss

Rank values then write about number 1

Be *grateful*
– once weekly
– 5 grateful things
– boosts happiness, too

Imagine eating
– curbs consumption
– savoury or sweet!
  – cinema!
  – buffets!
  – any time!

Approach > avoidance
– pursue do's NOT don'ts
– aspire to achieve

Plan in ƎSЯƎVƎᴚ
– work backwards in time

Motivation/ goals

Specific goals > broad goals
– link to depression?
– '*if … then*' implementation intentions

Empower refusal
– say 'don't' → feel in control
– say 'can't' → someone else is in control
– resist temptation
– say to other people

Track the g–a–p NOT progress
– stay dissatisfied

Reframe/reclaim pejorative names/labels
– 'sticks and stones may break my bones'

Stress is PERCEIVED
– how you *think/feel*

Physical and psychological effects

Avoid expressing emotion
– talk about passion, not emotion

Stress

Meaning/purpose
– future
– writing reduces cortisol
– up to 3 months' benefit
– write ✓
– talk ✗

Ecphory
– cues → positive memories
– e.g. photos
– fMRI benefits

Email
– CHECK LESS
– switching costs

A week later, all of the participants returned to the laboratory for a final exam to assess how much they had learnt. So which techniques do you think led to the best results?

If you read about the four groups again, I'm sure you can see that the first study group who only had five minutes' exposure to the materials were significantly hampered. After all, the other groups got to see the text for significantly longer. And on the final exam, these participants got scores of only 27%.

Remember that participants in the second group got to pore over their study materials in four sessions lasting five minutes each. Unsurprisingly then, these participants did significantly better on the test and scored 49% in the exam.

What kind of boost do you think the group got who drew out their own concept maps? After all, this group had to not only read the text but also understand the relationship between ideas enough to draw a diagram to represent them.

Perhaps surprisingly, though, the concept mapping participants only scored 45%. Creating a concept map was no more beneficial than simply reading the text over and over again.

The fourth and final group had only been allowed to read the materials for 10 minutes in total. However, they had spent twice as long – 20 minutes – being forced to recall whatever they could about the sea otters. And it was this group that performed the best. In the final exam, these participants scored an impressive 67%.[3]

In other words, if you want to learn something well, don't just read and re-read it. Don't bother with making fancy diagrams either. Instead, to fix something in your memory, test yourself on whatever you're trying to memorize. In fact, test yourself on it repeatedly, as the science shows that you will help yourself to remember it better in the long run.

> To fix something in your memory, test yourself on
> whatever you're trying to memorize.

Focusing on outputting rather than inputting

Psychologists talk about memory as involving at least two processes. Encoding (or what I prefer to call inputting) is the process of getting knowledge into your head by reading a book, watching a video or lecture, making notes or creating your own diagrams, and so on. In contrast, retrieval (or what I usually call outputting) is the part of the memory process that involves bringing information back out of storage so that you can use it – to take a written exam or teach someone else, for example.

The study by Karpicke and Blunt is massively important because it demonstrates that effective learning does not just involve encoding/inputting – trying to push information into your head. Instead, it's much better to spend the larger proportion of your time practising retrieval/outputting by testing, testing, and re-testing yourself.

A lot of people believe that learning is more about inputting than outputting. They think of inputting – cramming information into the brain – as the more important part of the equation. Indeed, a lot of people think of outputting as some passive process that merely involves regurgitating knowledge that's already there. But it's not. Outputting is an active process that reinforces memory and learning.

When I teach this research finding at conference events, I often liken the brain to a massive library. I say: think of your brain as a city-sized library made up of thousands of identical buildings, each of which is a hundred stories high. Just imagine row after unceasing row of these towering, yet indistinguishable buildings. Every floor of every building has hundreds of rooms. And each room is filled with thousands of old-fashioned metal filing cabinets.

Now imagine that inputting — learning something for the first time — is like having a mental filing clerk, sort of a little elf, typing some notes onto a sheet of paper and then slotting it into a folder, which needs to be put away into one of these rooms, on a floor of one of these buildings. Fine, it's been encoded.

But when you want to recall that information, you have to send one of your little filing clerks on a journey around your memory city to go to the right building, locate the correct floor, and not only get to the precise room but then also find the right filing cabinet, folder, and sheet of paper within it.

The danger is that the information is somewhere in a folder. But your filing clerk can't remember where. So it is lost to you forever.

But the way to find it again is by outputting and training that mental filing clerk to remember where she put that sheet of paper. And the more times you output, the more practised that filing clerk gets at finding exactly where it's located.

Research into the importance of outputting has been around for a long time. I remember reading about these sorts of studies when I was an undergraduate psychologist in my final year at university. When it came time to revise for my final exams, yes, I did spend time reading textbooks, poring over journal articles, and making notes. But I spent much, much more time testing myself. I forced myself to write full essays in response to real exam questions that had been asked in previous years. And when I ran out of past papers, I made up my own exam questions and wrote out full essays for those, too. I probably spent 10 or 20 times as much time on outputting as inputting.

As a result, I never felt terribly stressed during those final exams. I did nine hours of essay writing every day – trying not only to recall information but also to form it into a set of structured arguments. And when it came to those finals, I felt pretty confident. Ultimately, I came away with a first class honours degree (which I mention not to brag but as proof that doing a lot of retrieval/outputting certainly worked for me).

You may or may not have to do written exams in your future. But think about applying this research to other areas of your life. For instance, you may want to learn enough of a foreign language so you can get by on a holiday. Or you may need to memorize a speech to give at a wedding or a presentation to deliver at work. Whatever your situation, spend less time inputting and a lot more time outputting.

> Whatever your situation, spend less time inputting and a lot more time outputting.

As a final example, when I'm preparing to give a speech at a conference, I spend a little bit of time scribbling notes and working out the main points that I'd like to make. But then I practise delivering the talk over and over again. I probably spend three or four times as long on outputting – actually rehearsing my speech out loud – as I do on writing the speech in the first place.

Learning by sounding off

Personally, I've never been able to get into audiobooks. Even when I had laser eye surgery a few years ago (to correct short-sightedness) and was told to recuperate in a darkened room with my eyes closed for a day, I found it hard to concentrate on listening to an audiobook. But I know that more than a few friends and clients listen to business or self-improvement audiobooks and see it as a good way to learn. But is it really a good way to learn?

Psychological scientists Noah Forrin and Colin MacLeod from the University of Waterloo in Canada designed an experiment to test the effects of the written versus spoken word in boosting memory. But they also had a couple of questions that they wished to test. When listening to the spoken word, would it matter *who* said it? Specifically, if you were to hear material being read out in your *own* voice as opposed to a stranger's voice, would that make a difference?

The researchers started their experiment by asking 75 participants to enter a recording studio to read out loud a list of 160 nouns. Two weeks later, everybody was invited back to study and memorize the nouns. They were then tested on how many they could remember. However, the participants were split into four groups.

- The first group sat and studied the word list in silence. So even though they had initially read out loud the whole list in the recording studio, this time they were asked to memorize the words in silence.

- A second group listened to a playback of the word list, but being read out by two experimenters. As with all of the other participants, they had initially read aloud the words. But now they heard the words being played back in other people's voices.

- The third group listened to their own audio recordings.

- A fourth group were shown the words again and asked to read them out loud for a second time. The researchers included this additional group as they wondered whether actively reading out words would affect memory differently from passively listening to words.[4]

So did the spoken word beat reading in silence? Yes. The researchers found that participants in the second group who listened to strangers' recordings performed better in the memory test than the participants in the first group who merely read in silence.

That's good news then if you're a fan of audiobooks. Listening to someone else reciting material may actually boost your learning more than when reading it silently.

But the researchers found that the third group who listened to their own voices performed even better. And this was exactly what Forrin and MacLeod had expected, as most people tend to be somewhat self-interested – they seem to pay more attention to their own voices than other people's voices. So when you hear yourself reading something out loud, that material gets more deeply embedded into your memory.

> When you hear yourself reading something out loud, that material gets more deeply embedded into your memory.

But it was the fourth group who performed best in the memory test. Why? Well, these participants did not just passively read words in silence. Neither did they passively hear words being read out to them. No, these people looked at the words *and* had to move muscles in their faces and necks in order to articulate the words out loud. *And* they heard the words through their ears. *And* the words they heard were in their own voices. It was a quadruple whammy.

Harnessing the production effect

The production effect gets its name from the fact that saying words out loud tends to result in better memory than simply reading them silently. Of course, circumstances may often dictate that you can't read out loud. For example, if you're driving a car, it would be incredibly dangerous to try to read a book. And if you're on a train or a plane, other passengers are probably not going to be terribly enthusiastic if you start reading out loud.

More broadly, though, remember the hierarchy of learning methods, listed in order from least to most effective:

● Reading silently (least effective)

● Listening to someone else reading

● Listening to yourself reading

● Reading aloud (most effective)

The implication should be clear. Whether you're a sales person who needs to memorize your company's product range or a student revising for an exam, make the most of your time by reading out loud.

Looking at the hierarchy of learning methods, then, an audio-book may indeed be a better way to absorb information than simply reading something silently by yourself. But you could get an even bigger boost to your learning if you listen to your-self reading a book. Yes, it would be time-consuming to record yourself. But suppose you're revising for an exam and keen to make the best use of every minute while commuting. In a situation like that, recording yourself reading material out loud could be a pretty good idea so that you can listen to it again and again. Given the quality of most smartphones, that should actually be very easy to do.

However, remember that the biggest boost to learning comes from reading aloud – the so-called production effect. It's the most involving method. You don't just skim your eyes over words on a page. You have to activate muscles in order to pronounce every word. Plus you get to hear the words. And it's not just anybody's voice, but your own, too.

That makes total sense to me. For example, clients have for years been asking me to shoot short training videos for them on topics such as emotional intelligence, leadership, and motivation. For each video, I write a script of perhaps 600 to 1,000 words in length and then rehearse it over and over again – usually around a half-dozen times – until I have committed the whole script to memory. And whenever I rehearse, I always read out loud. I've always found it more beneficial to read the script out loud than to read in silence.

So our second technique for boosting your learning and memory is based on the so-called production effect. Reading aloud only requires a little more effort than reading silently. But it's effort that measurably pays off in the end.

> Remember that the biggest boost to learning comes from reading aloud – the so-called production effect.

I actually integrate this into workshops. For example, I ran a workshop for around 50 lawyers recently on how to use emotional intelligence to win over clients. The workshop lasted three hours and about every 20 to 30 minutes, I gave them a break in which they had to write down bullet points for the main points that we had covered. They did this individually, in silence. In pairs, they then talked through what they thought were the key lessons.

This had multiple benefits. It wasn't just me droning on at them for several hours. But more importantly, they had to test themselves (by writing down what they thought they had learnt) *and* tell someone else about it.

Making learning difficult

So far we've talked about learning in the context of memorizing scripts for presentations or perhaps material for exams. But what if you're trying to learn a physical skill – say a new sport or a musical instrument?

Imagine that you've never played tennis before but have just made a bet that you can learn enough in six months to beat a friend in a tennis match. Your friend isn't an expert. In fact, she only started playing a year ago. So you think you have a sporting chance.

You hire a coach who suggests that you should focus your early lessons on just three main shots: the forehand, the back-hand, and the smash. Your coach then asks you: how would you like to structure your hour-long sessions? Would you prefer to spend 20 minutes on forehands, then 20 minutes on backhands, and finally 20 minutes on smashes? That way, you get to con-centrate on each shot.

Or would you prefer to mix things up and have to cope with a less predictable combination of shots – perhaps a couple of forehands, a smash, a few more forehands, and then a barrage of backhands? This option would provide you with more variety – but perhaps there's a risk of more confusion, too.

Essentially, the question is whether you would prefer distinct blocks of practice for each skill or for the different skills to be intermingled – or, to use the technical psychological term, interleaved. Of course, this is a hypothetical situation for you, but a very real concern in the world of sports. It's a question that has been debated and investigated for decades by sports coaches and performance directors all over the world. After all, if you can train a football, basketball, or baseball team in a way that helps them to refine their skills more quickly, that's the kind of training method that could help your team to make real money in prizes and sponsorship deals.

One of the first studies to investigate the effectiveness of the different training methods was run in the 1980s by Louisiana State University investigators Sinah Goode and Richard Magill. The two sport scientists recruited 30 students who were willing to be taught three different types of badminton serve: the short serve, the long serve, and the drive serve.

All of the participants took part in nine training sessions of 36 serves per session. But the participants were split into three groups, which were taught the serves in slightly different ways.

The first group practised in blocks that involved practising only one shot per session. For example, they may have practised 36 short serves on Monday, 36 long serves on Wednesday, and 36 drive serves on Friday.

The second group were taught all three shots in each session, but in a predictable sequence every day. So, irrespective of the day of the week, they might have done one short serve, then a long serve, followed by a drive serve – then repeated this over and over again until they had completed 36 serves in the session.

The final group were forced to intermingle their shots in a random sequence. So these participants also completed 36 serves, but they might have done one short serve, three drive serves, two long serves, another short serve, and so on.

At the end of the several weeks of training, all of the participants were asked to perform the three serves under strictly monitored test conditions. The researchers wanted to see which group had learnt to perform the three serves the most accurately.

One way of reframing the question is to consider: did the random teaching order confuse the participants and result in poorer performance? Or did it challenge them more deeply and result in better performance?

Care to place a bet on which was better?

The sport scientists found that the completely random order produced the best levels of performance – surpassing both the blocked teaching method and the mixed but predictable sequences. In other words, the most effective way to learn seemed to involve interleaving the three skills in a random fashion.[5]

Since that ground-breaking study, other researchers have similarly observed the greater benefits of intermingled practice over blocked practice. For example, researchers Christine Carter from Memorial University of Newfoundland and Jessica Grahn from Western University found that musicians (clarinet players) who were taught new pieces of music did better when they alternated between pieces rather than learning them in blocks, one at a time.[6]

So for sports and musical talents, interleaving may be a pretty good idea. But how about when it comes to classroom studies or the sort of skills that help people to do their jobs in the workplace?

Some studies have similarly found that interleaving worked well. For instance, one group of researchers taught school students to solve fairly difficult mathematical puzzles in either blocked or intermingled lessons. Two weeks after the course ended, all of the students took an exam. Students taught using blocked practice scored on average 38%. But students taught using intermingled practice scored a massive 72%.[7] Clearly that suggests a huge advantage for interleaved learning.

However, other studies have found the opposite result. For example, a different group of researchers taught undergraduate medical students the skill of electrocardiogram (ECG) interpretation using either blocked or interleaved practice sessions. The medical students were taught to scrutinize ECG reports in order to identify medical conditions such as pericarditis and ischaemia.

When the students were later tested on their interpretation skills, those who studied in blocks scored 34% in the exam. Unfortunately, those who had been taught in the interleaved sessions only managed to score 24%.[8]

OK. So interleaving helped maths students but led to worse results for medical students. What can we conclude from this?

For the time being, we can't say exactly how interleaving may benefit or otherwise affect the acquisition of more complex mental skills. The research is ongoing and it may turn out that interleaving is more effective for certain mental skills but less effective for others.

Or it may be that not everybody learns academic skills in the same way. For instance, very new research suggests that people may learn best when they get to choose how long to spend on different concepts. Scientists led by Indiana University's Paulo Carvalho found that psychology students who got to choose their own study blocks got significantly higher exam scores than students who had study blocks imposed on them.[9] When it comes to learning mental and scholastic skills, then, my advice is to schedule your study time using whatever combination of blocks and interleaving makes the most sense to you.

> When it comes to learning mental and scholastic skills, then, my advice is to schedule your study time using whatever combination of blocks and interleaving makes the most sense to you.

However, interleaving still has its uses. The evidence does suggest that interleaving benefits people who wish to learn physical and musical skills. So perhaps it's a technique that you can apply to your passions more than to your professional life.

> Interleaving benefits people who wish to learn physical and musical skills.

Interleaving your learning

In multiple studies, scientists have found that people who learn new sporting or musical skills in intermingled practice sessions tend to do better than people who try to learn in simpler blocks. Suppose you have to learn four skills, which we'll call A, B, C, and D. A simple, blocked practice schedule might involve tackling A multiple times first (AAAAAAAA) before moving on to B (BBBBBBBB), and so on. But an intermingled schedule would involve tackling the four skills in a serial fashion (ABCDABCD) and then maybe even a different order later on (say BADCBADC).

The evidence for the benefits of interleaving for more academic or mental skills is mixed. Perhaps the point for these skills is that there is more than one way to study. Rather than cover one topic in its entirety, it may help *some* people to learn in smaller chunks. For example, suppose you're studying for a professional exam and want to study for three hours every week night. You might initially decide to study two topics each time for 90 minutes each. But someone else might prefer to study three topics for an hour each. And another student might prefer to dedicate the full three hours to just the one topic. So maybe run an experiment trying out different ways to spend your time to see to what extent interleaving versus blocking may work for you.

There is one drawback to the interleaved learning method. When learning physical or musical skills, the process of inter-mingled learning can feel more difficult. It may tax you more physically and mentally. After all, when you practise just one skill at a time (AAAAAAAA before moving on to BBBBBBBB), it's easier to feel that you have mastered each skill properly. When you're tackling the skills in a seemingly random order (say ABBDCEECAD), it's easier to feel confused or even over-whelmed by the scale of having to learn so many new and dif-ferent skills at once. So there's a trade-off. Learning new skills through interleaving feels more challenging – it requires more effort in the short-term. But it may ultimately pay off through better results in the long-term.

> Learning new skills through interleaving feels more challenging – it requires more effort in the short-term.

Applying asymmetric activation

Let's finish this chapter with something that may seem a bit quirky to begin with. But I'll start with some background on the topic first.

Given that you are reading a book on psychology, you are probably aware that the brain is separated into two sides, or hemispheres, which tend to control physical movement on opposite sides of the body. The left hemisphere is responsible for actions on the right side of the body; the right hemisphere directs movement on the left side. Medical researchers know this for a fact, because a stroke on one side of the brain often leads to movement problems or even paralysis on the opposite side of the body.

Each hemisphere is also responsible for certain mental tasks. For example, people who suffer a stroke in the left hemisphere are more likely to experience difficulties with speech and language than those who have a stroke in the right hemisphere. In contrast, people who have a stroke in the right hemisphere more often struggle with spatial judgements than those who have strokes on the left side.

But how does this relate to learning, exactly?

Given the different tasks performed by each hemisphere, a team of memory researchers led by Montclair State University scientist Ruth Propper hypothesized that each hemisphere may have a different role in learning and memory. So they recruited 50 adults for an experiment in which the participants had different hemispheres of the brain stimulated while learning and then being tested on their recall of a list of 36 words.

To provide a baseline for their results, Propper and her team asked a control group of participants to learn and then be tested on their recall of the words with no hemispheric stimulation. During the test, this group on average recalled 7.6 words correctly.

Four further groups of participants had one hemisphere stimulated before being presented with the words they were asked to learn; they then had either the same or a different hemisphere stimulated before being tested on their recall. So these four groups were as follows:

- Right hemisphere learning, right hemisphere recall
- Right hemisphere learning, left hemisphere recall

- Left hemisphere learning, left hemisphere recall
- Left hemisphere learning, right hemisphere recall

Counting up the numbers of correctly recalled words, the researchers found that the group who had their left hemisphere stimulated before learning and then the right hemisphere stimulated before the test performed more strongly, recalling 9.1 words on average. Given that the control group recalled 7.6 words, a difference of 1.5 words may not seem terribly impressive. But that actually represents a 19.9% improvement. Just imagine getting 19.9% more marks in a test or exam.

The other hemispheric stimulation groups scored much worse, with recall as low as 4.7 words for one group. But the important point here is that left-hemisphere stimulation before learning and then right-hemisphere stimulation before recall may result in the best performance.

> Left-hemisphere stimulation before learning and then right-hemisphere stimulation before recall may result in the best performance.

Ah. But perhaps you're wondering how you can stimulate each hemisphere of the brain. After all, it wouldn't be terribly practical to have to shove electrodes into your brain every time you wanted to learn or recall anything.

Remember that the brain tends to control movement on the opposite side of the body? Well, the effect actually works both ways: physical activity on one side of the body can also stimulate the opposite hemisphere.

So participants who were asked to clench their right hands were able to activate their left hemispheres. And participants who clenched their left hands stimulated their right hemispheres.

It really is that straightforward. Participants who squeezed their right hands (and activated their left hemispheres) before seeing a list of words were better able to learn – or encode, to use the psychological parlance – those words. When these participants then squeezed their left hands (activating their right hemispheres) before being tested for their recall, they enhanced their ability to retrieve those same words from memory.[10]

Using HERA to boost your memory and learning

The two hemispheres of the brain contribute in different ways during the processes of learning (encoding) and recall. Researchers such as Ruth Propper and her colleagues describe this as hemispheric encoding/retrieval asymmetry (HERA).

But you don't have to memorize the theory behind the method, only how to use it. If you want to encode (learn or input) material more effectively, clench your right hand into a fist beforehand. When you need to retrieve (output) that material, simply clench your left hand into a fist before you need to recall whatever it was that you had to learn.

I realize I've talked a lot about the different hemispheres. But remember that one side of the body is linked to the opposite hemisphere of the brain. So don't worry too much about the hemispheres. Just remember the practical implication. Clench your right hand before learning and clench your left hand when you need to bring it back to mind.

Or, early on in the chapter, I mentioned that I tend to refer to learning or encoding as inputting. In contrast, retrieving or recalling is outputting. So how about using the acronym RILO for right input, left output? Perhaps that will remind you to clench right to input and clench left to output.

> Clench your right hand before learning and clench your left hand when you need to bring it back to mind.

Onwards and upwards

- Remember the difference between inputting and outputting when it comes to learning. Inputting information simply by reading and rereading material is not a terribly effective way to learn and memorize it. Even taking notes and drawing diagrams isn't that useful. To make better use of your time, devote a significant proportion of it to outputting. Test yourself repeatedly: see how much you can recall over and over, then over and over again.

- When you are beginning to learn new material, consider reading it out loud. Remember that moving your mouth and generating words out loud seems to embed information more deeply in your brain. Or, if it's not convenient to read aloud, consider recording yourself reading materials out loud so that you can listen to them later – you still get a significant bump in your learning as compared with simply reading something in silence.

- If you're trying to learn physical (e.g. sporting) or musical skills, consider mixing up your practice sessions. Yes, it may feel easier to learn one skill at a time. However, bear in mind the research on intermingling: mixing up different skills may help to improve your performance when you ultimately need to give of your best in, say, a competition or audition.

- For an almost immediate boost to your memory, remember the HERA (hemispheric encoding/retrieval asymmetry) effect. To encode (i.e. learn or input) information more effectively, clench your right hand. And to help yourself to retrieve (i.e. recall or output) that same information, clench your left hand.

7

Dealing with pressure and performing in public

'Always do what you are afraid to do.'

Ralph Waldo Emerson

A client of mine called Christopher is a rocket scientist. Well, he has several degrees in chemistry. And for his doctorate he specialized in research on hydrogen fuel cells. He couldn't build a rocket on his own. But he'd sure be an asset if you really were planning on sending a spaceship to Mars.

Up until his late 30s, Christopher worked as a scientist for a large German chemical company. Unfortunately, changing times led to his entire division being sold off. And he found himself out of a job.

He couldn't find work in pure research. So he changed direction by taking a job as a university lecturer.

He was still able to do some research. He also quite enjoyed marking assignments and exam papers. However, he found it fairly nerve-wracking having to lecture to students every day.

And so he came to me for help. When we first met, Christopher had already been lecturing for about a month. He said that having to lecture meant that his whole body was pretty much drenched in sweat – he had to wear a t-shirt under his shirt every day in order to mop up the perspiration that burst from him. He was completely preoccupied by the dryness in his throat and mouth; he spent a lot of time gulping down water in an attempt to stay hydrated. Worst of all, he was sure that his students were able to detect his anxiety.

Of course, many, many people feel nervous about the prospect of having to get up in front of an audience. Imagine moving to the front of a large auditorium. There could be around a hundred pairs of eyes looking at you. Maybe a dozen or so people are chatting to each other, yawning, checking their phones, even pointing and giggling at you or otherwise giving the impression that they find you less than entirely enthralling. And that's before you have to give your presentation to them, which could last up to two or three *hours*.

Yes, lots of people hate even the idea of having to give a speech or presentation. Not just lecturing, but giving a talk to colleagues or even a speech perhaps at a party or wedding banquet. Thankfully, science tells us that there are quite a few tweaks that can help people like Christopher as well as you to perform better in public.

> Many, many people feel nervous about the prospect of having to get up in front of an audience.

Activating your autobiographical armour

If you're one of the many millions of people worldwide who hates the prospect of having to give a speech in public, think back to your earlier years. Can you ever remember a time in your life when you were *not* afraid to stand up and speak in front of other people?

Your initial answer may be 'no' – you may think that you have always been anxious about performing in public. But I'd suggest taking a little more time to think about it, because recalling an earlier, positive public speaking experience could just form the basis of a performance-enhancing technique.

Some years ago, a research team led by Murray Stein – who at the time was a young psychological scientist at the University of California, San Diego – carried out one of the most comprehensive surveys of public speaking fears that has ever been done. The researchers conducted telephone interviews with a sample of nearly 500 adults and found that nearly one in three people said that they experienced 'excessive anxiety' over having to speak in front of a large audience. Many of these people worried about doing or saying something embarrassing, having their mind go blank and even trembling or showing other physical signs of their anxiety.

More importantly, though, nearly all of these individuals were able to identify more or less the age when such worries began. Ninety per cent of the people who felt excessively troubled about public speaking said that these fears had emerged by the age of 20. Seventy-five per cent of them thought that these anxieties surfaced by the age of 17. And 50% of them believed that they had picked up their worries by the age of 13.[1]

In other words, the further back in time people went, the more likely they were to recall a time when they did *not* feel apprehensive about having to speak in public. Go back enough years and there is often a time when most people felt OK about speaking in front of others. They may even have enjoyed it.

> Go back enough years and there is often a time when most people felt OK about speaking in front of others.

But how does this help us to perform better?

For the answer, we turn to a later experiment conducted by Kathy Pezdek and Roxanna Salim, a research duo at Claremont Graduate University in California. The pioneering scientists decided to try to alleviate public speaking anxiety in teenage students at two local high schools.

All of the students were asked to prepare and then deliver a five-minute speech in front of a live audience. These brave – or perhaps hapless – students were told that they would be evaluated on their communication skills. That was already fairly nerve-wracking but, to add to the pressure, they were told that their performances would be filmed and later scrutinized by a separate group of experts.

Just before giving their presentations, though, the students were split into two groups. The first (experimental) group were told that they were likely to have experienced some positive public speaking experiences before the age of 10. They were given five minutes to think about one of these experiences and write down as much as they could remember about that particular situation.

These students were not told that they were good at public speaking. They were only told that they were likely to have had some kind of positive public speaking experience – perhaps speaking to friends, classmates, or even just members of their own family.

The second (control) group were told that they were likely to have experienced some other positive experiences before the age of 10. These students were also given five minutes to recall one of these experiences and to write about it.

Both groups of students completed questionnaires asking them to say how anxious they felt. That's pretty standard in these sorts of studies. But the students' filmed speeches were later also watched and scored by a panel of three experts.

When the researchers analysed their data, they found that the students who had written about a positive public speaking situation in childhood fared significantly better. Writing about a positive, related experience enabled them to feel better psychologically and their performances were rated more highly by the independent observers.[2]

That's important because the autobiographical technique didn't just help the students with their inward stress, their feelings.

It also made a demonstrable difference to their outward behaviour and how they were perceived by other people.

The study is also commendable for the fact that the researchers included a control group – in which participants recalled an unrelated memory. This showed that simply recalling *something* is not enough. It's not just the fact that the participants engaged in some kind of distracting activity. Only being prompted to recall a *positive, related* childhood memory helps to lift one's performance.

> Being prompted to recall a positive, related childhood memory helps to lift one's performance.

So there we have it: scientific support that taking a few minutes to recall a positive, relevant childhood experience could be an effective method for warding off anxiety and boosting performance. Care to give it a try?

Recalling past positive experiences

To summarize, research suggests that many people who develop particular fears may do so in their teenage years. However, researchers found that recalling a related childhood positive experience – specifically one that occurred before the age of 10 – was effective at not only reducing psychological stress but also boosting performance. If you want to lift your performance using this autobiographical technique, you may want to bear in mind the following tips based on the research:

- Pick a *specific* earlier, positive experience that is related to the situation that you are about to face. Think back to this one instance, this one particular situation, rather than thinking about how you *generally* used to behave.

- *Write* in as much detail as you can about your past positive experience. Simply trying to recall the situation in your head may not work as well.

- Spend a full five minutes writing about this earlier incident or situation. And remember to do this writing exercise before whatever anxiety-provoking or otherwise challenging event you're getting ready to face.

Before we move on, I'd like to distinguish between this technique and one that we encountered at the start of the book. Back in Chapter 1, we looked at a study by researchers Megan Speer and Mauricio Delgado involving the ecphory – or cued recall – of happy memories. These researchers found that using a cue to trigger happy memories helped people to recover more quickly *after* they had been made to feel stressed.

In contrast, Kathy Pezdek and Roxanna Salim found that asking people to write about a related childhood positive experience helped to shield them during a subsequent challenge. So this technique differs from ecphory in three ways. First of all, it is a written exercise (whereas ecphory just involves mentally replaying happier times). Secondly, it benefits not only people's anxiety levels but also their performance as observed by other people. Thirdly (and perhaps most importantly), it has its protective effects when used *before* encountering a tough situation.

So yes, both of these techniques involve recalling positive events from the past. But they are not exactly the same. They differ not only in their methods but also in their effects.

Using the body–mind connection

If you watch a lot of sport – whether that's football or tennis, gymnastics or track and field – you have probably noticed a lot of athletes wearing strips of coloured tape on their bodies. This physiotherapy tape is designed to hold muscles in certain positions in order to aid performance and reduce the likelihood of injury.

Sure, it may help muscles to work more effectively – it may affect physical performance. But could being taped up have any effects on cognitive performance, too?

Imagine for a moment that you've agreed to take part in yet another research investigation. You arrive at a suite of offices and a research assistant – a young man in a white lab coat – explains: 'People who visit physiotherapists sometimes report effects from tape placed on their backs in their daily physical, mental, and social tasks. This study is to investigate the effects of tape on your upper back on your physiology, mood, and performance of a speech task.'

You're asked to sit on a stool with a relaxed back and shoulders so that your spine curves forwards, your chin is nearly on your chest, and your shoulders slump forwards. He then attaches physiotherapy tape across your back – it's a bit cold for a few seconds against your bare skin but you soon get used to it and the somewhat slouched position you're in.

Then the experiment begins properly. You're asked to imagine that you're about to be interviewed for your dream job. You now have five minutes to prepare a short speech. Your speech must last five minutes and you should tell an interview panel why you're the best candidate for the job. Your performance will be recorded on camera for later scrutiny by several interviewers and the best candidate from all of the participants in the study will win a shopping voucher worth £200.

So you give your presentation. Perhaps during your speech, you can feel your heart racing. But hey, it's natural to feel a bit nervous, right?

Afterwards, you are given a couple of questionnaires to complete. You're asked to rate how you're feeling on a five-point scale ranging from 1 for 'very slightly or not at all' to 5 for 'extremely'. You work your way through a list of adjectives and tick the extent to which you're feeling 'enthusiastic', 'sleepy', 'nervous', 'happy', and a bunch of others.

And that's all there is to it. Thank you very much for your participation.

This was essentially the experimental protocol used by researchers led by Shwetha Nair at the University of Auckland in New Zealand. Except they weren't really investigating the effects of physiotherapy tape on performance. They were looking at the effects of posture – they merely used the tape as a cover story to stop participants from guessing that the study was actually about the impact of posture on psychological performance. Essentially, the researchers believed that the posture of the body could have real effects on the mind.

> The posture of the body could have real effects on the mind.

One group of participants was asked to assume a slouched posture during the tests. But a second group was asked to assume an upright posture – with a straight back and shoulder blades pulled back.

And the researchers discovered that the two postures did indeed have markedly different effects during the series of tests. The upright participants felt significantly more enthusiastic, excited, and strong; the slumped participants reported feeling more nervous, passive, dull, sleepy, sluggish, and even more hostile and fearful. The upright participants also reported measurably higher levels of self-esteem than those who sat in the slouched position.

Clearly then, posture had a real impact on people's feelings during their speeches. Sitting upright helped people to feel decidedly better.

But the researchers also conducted another level of analysis. They asked a team of experts to watch every video, painstakingly making notes of the types of words that each participant used. Again, there was a noticeable difference here. The upright participants used more positive emotion words and fewer negative emotion words; they also used more words in total, which seemed to indicate that they were just more energized, full stop.[3]

There's more. The benefits of better posture may not just relate to speaking in public either. In a more recent study, researchers jointly from San Francisco State University and Kaohsiung Medical University in Taiwan asked 125 adults to perform a mathematics task while either slumped forwards or sitting upright. No prizes for guessing that participants who sat upright found the task significantly easier.[4]

The list goes on. Scientists led by Lotte Veenstra at VU University Amsterdam found that having a straight posture allowed people to recover more quickly from bad moods.[5] And yet another study by German researchers even suggests that walking around with a more upright posture may help to fend off depression, too.

Overall, it's such a simple intervention that I almost can't believe it works. But it does. Research conducted all over the world confirms that an upright posture seems to have multiple benefits. Remember that an upright posture doesn't just change how people feel. It alters how much they talk and the amount of positivity they convey in their speech. And it may even make mental calculations easier to perform, too.

My final thought on the topic is a reflection on my childhood. When I was growing up, my parents frequently told me to sit or stand up straight – whether I was studying or watching TV or just walking around. It looks like they were very right to do so!

> Research conducted all over the world confirms that an upright posture seems to have multiple benefits.

Changing your bodily state to boost mental performance

How would you describe your posture right now? Whether you're sitting or standing, are you doing so with your head forwards and a relaxed but maybe slumped posture? Or are your shoulders back, chest out and head high?

Research clearly shows that people who hold their bodies in an upright fashion perform more strongly under pressure. That's very simple to understand. But the trick here is *remembering* to use it.

If I were working with you as a client, I would be encouraging you right now to think of the handful of upcoming situations in which you could use this tweak. So what kind of pressurized scenarios may be coming up in the near future? Maybe some are to do with conversations or confrontations you need to have with other people. Perhaps some are to do with complex tasks that will tax your intelligence or patience.

Then, think about how you will remind yourself to implement this advice. Would writing a note or two in your diary be helpful? Maybe a reminder on your phone? Or a sticky note on the side of your computer screen?

Ensuring that you have a strong, upright posture may help you to not only make a better impact but also feel and think more strongly. Try it.

Choosing to see things differently

If you're a long-time follower of English football, the name Chris Waddle – especially in conjunction with the 1990 football World Cup – will forever be a bitter memory. Playing for England in the semi-final against Germany, he missed a penalty. Millions of English football fans groaned, moaned, and shouted at their televisions as he kicked the ball completely over the top of the net – pundits have joked that the ball is probably still in orbit.

How could he possibly have missed? He started playing football professionally at the age of 19. He was 30 years old by the time of the infamous World Cup match – so he had been playing professionally for 11 years. Just imagine how many penalty kicks he had taken or practised in his career.

But he missed. And the incident is one of sport's most notorious examples of what is popularly referred to as choking, choking under pressure, or sometimes the yips. Psychologists typically refer to it in more neutral language – for example calling it motor skill failure. But it amounts to the same thing: the breakdown of even highly practised skills in the face of intense pressure.

You can find examples of performance choking in almost every sport all over the planet: world class tennis players who fell apart when it should have been their chance to shine and Olympic gymnasts who landed face-first despite having performed their manoeuvres many thousands of times previously. Then there are golfers, boxers, figure skaters, baseball players, snowboarders – the list goes on.

> You can find examples of performance choking in almost every sport all over the planet.

It doesn't just happen to high achieving athletes either. It can happen to just about anybody. Singers and musicians practise for years but sometimes mess up when they get to important auditions or competitions. I've seen more than a few presenters embarrass themselves in front of audiences – despite having rehearsed a lot beforehand and being unequalled experts in their fields. And there are plenty of talented, qualified job hunters who freeze and end up garbling their stories when it comes to jobs that they really want.

When people choke, it's not that they have not practised or rehearsed enough. It's more the pressure that gets to them: the thought that they are on the cusp of a vital win, a big breakthrough, or the opportunity that they so desperately want.

It's actually surprisingly easy to make people go wrong: it doesn't take that much pressure. Dutch researchers led by Yannick Balk at Utrecht University once invited experienced golfers to take part in an experiment involving golf putting. Using standard golf balls and regular putters, the golfers were asked to putt 10 balls into a hole across a distance of around two metres. When there was no pressure, they on average putted 6.3 balls.

But then the experimenters ramped up the stakes. They told the golfers that the next 10 putts would be filmed for later analysis; they also said that the golfers' scores would be published on a noticeboard in their clubhouse.

The thing is, these participants had on average been playing golf for nearly 22 years. They were only participating in a little psychology experiment. There was no huge prize money at stake. The worst that could happen would be that their pride might be slightly dented. It really shouldn't have mattered. But it did. And their performance dropped to 5.0 putts on average.

A drop from 6.3 to 5.0 putts may not seem like a big deal. But that's a drop in performance of 20.6%. Clearly, that's a huge margin – the difference between a win and a crushing defeat – when it matters.

Now, the researchers thought that they could train golfers to protect themselves from choking. So they taught other golfers a tiny psychological tactic for immunizing them against pressure. They told these golfers:

> We would like to see to what extent you can control the way you experience things. Therefore, it is very important to us that you try your best to adopt a positive attitude towards putting the golf ball. For example, keep reminding yourself that putting the golf ball is just a game.

And it worked. When this group of players were exposed to more pressure, they didn't make any more mistakes. After this simple instruction, their performance stayed at the same level.[6]

Again, it's a fairly simple tactic, isn't it? Adopt a positive attitude. Remind yourself that it's just a game. Change your perspective on what's happening and you help yourself to perform at your best.

Change your perspective on what's happening and you help yourself to perform at your best.

Adopting a more positive point of view

Choking happens when practised people underperform in the face of high pressure. Here's the thing, though: pressure is an extremely subjective quality. Some athletes and performers don't feel pressure even when they're performing in front of tens of thousands of people. But others may feel anxious and panicky even if it's just one job interviewer or a small audience of a half-dozen supportive colleagues in front of them.

You know yourself best. So figure out when you feel under pressure. And when that happens, try to adopt a more positive attitude.

Rather than focusing on why you feel threatened or what you might lose, reframe the challenge in a more helpful manner. Remind yourself that the people in front of you are just... people. They're no different from you or me. Or tell yourself that it's only an audition, presentation, performance, or game – you won't actually die. Whatever happens, the sun will still rise tomorrow.

You could maybe imagine how a good friend might encourage you to see the situation. Or imagine how disinterested and unbothered by pressure a young child trying the task might be. There's no right answer here. It's just about coming up with a more positive point of view, a different way of looking at the challenge that feels more advantageous to you.

Using rituals to boost performance

Still on the topic of sports, Spanish tennis player Rafael Nadal is one of the most decorated tennis players of all time in terms of the number of grand slam tournaments he has won. With that comes a certain amount of financial success: he has earned prize money well in excess of $100 million. Just to put that into perspective, if he were to retire any time soon – and assuming he invested his earnings – he would probably be able to live off around $4 million a year *for the rest of his life*.

What makes Nadal one of the greatest players of all time? Perhaps it has something to do with his pre-match rituals.

When getting dressed in the locker room before a match, he puts on his socks and checks that both are exactly the same height on his calves. And then he puts his trademark bandanna on his head, tying it on slowly and carefully. It's not just a way of keeping his hair out of his eyes – it's something that he does deliberately. It's part of his mental preparation for the physical confrontation to come.

Once on court, he sits down and takes a sip from a bottle of water. Then he takes a sip from a second bottle. And he repeats the sequence every time – not only before the match begins but also at every break between games until the match is over. A sip from one bottle, and then another sip from the other. When he puts his bottles down, he places the bottles at his feet in front of his chair and to his left, one neatly behind the other, so that the two are diagonally aimed at the court.

Writing in a British newspaper, Nadal once explained: 'It's a way of placing myself in a match, ordering my surroundings to match the order I seek in my head.'[7]

Nadal isn't the only athlete in the world with a pre-game ritual. Numerous tennis players, golfers, basketball players, figure skaters, and other athletes have their own rituals.

What about you? Do you have any rituals? Think about a time when you faced a difficult task or situation and you felt anxious about it. It may have been a test or an exam, a sporting competition, an interview or presentation, perhaps an audition or any other type of performance. Have you ever engaged in a ritual before the task or situation?

When a group of researchers led by Harvard University's Alison Wood Brooks surveyed 400 adults, they found that nearly half (46.5%) of people reported having performed some kind of ritual in a high-stakes situation. So if you have ever recited certain words to yourself, carried out any physical routine, or even relied on a lucky charm, you are in good company.

> Rituals actually work. They can measurably improve performance.

And here's the thing: *rituals actually work.* They can measurably improve performance. In one study, Brooks and her colleagues asked 85 people to take part in a singing test, which involved singing 'Don't Stop Believin'', a song by the group Journey, on a Nintendo game called Karaoke Revolution. Rather cleverly, the game monitors a singer's performance and calculates a singing accuracy score on a scale from zero to 100.

Half of the experimental participants spent a minute sitting quietly. But the other half were asked to engage in a completely made-up ritual. They were told:

> Draw a picture of how you are feeling right now. Sprinkle salt on your drawing. Count up to five out loud. Crinkle up your paper. Throw your paper in the trash.

The ritual was not based on rigorous psychological theory. Actually, it was something spurious that the researchers just made up. But it worked. While participants who sat quietly got singing accuracy scores of 65.7%, those who ran through the newly contrived ritual achieved scores of 78.4%.

That's a fairly impressive benefit from an inconsequential ritual – more than the 10% boost promised in the title of this book, for example. Oh, and the participants who drew the picture and completed the rest of the ritual also reported feeling significantly less anxious. So a ritual may not only boost performance – it helps people to feel more relaxed, too.

> A ritual may not only boost performance – it helps people to feel more relaxed, too.

In further studies, Alison Wood Brooks and her collaborators investigated other manufactured rituals, such as asking people to count out loud slowly from zero to 10 and then back down to zero again before sprinkling salt on a piece of paper. And because singing is a skill that involves performing in public, they tested how people performed in a written test of their mathematical ability, too. But the results continued to be positive: all sorts of rituals were helpful in not only public settings but also written exams.[8]

Crafting a routine that's right for you

Psychologists define a ritual as any fixed sequence of behaviours that lack overt functional purpose, but have a symbolic meaning. For example, an athlete may stretch or do sprints because these help to get the body warmed up for exercise – they have a functional purpose. In contrast, Rafael Nadal puts his water bottles on the left of his chair not because it helps him to hit a tennis ball harder but because it has a special meaning for him.

So a ritual can be just about anything *so long as it has a meaning for you*. If you like to carry a good luck token with you before job interviews or auditions, then go ahead. If you like to recite a mantra or do a haka, please continue to do so. It could be a ritual that has been passed down for generations – for example, people in Western countries commonly talk about 'knocking on wood' or throwing salt. Or it could be a ritual that you have created for yourself.

Your ritual could even be something that you perform with other people. Many sports teams as well as sales teams pump themselves up through inspirational chants. So there's no need to go it alone.

Whatever your ritual, the science says that it may genuinely pay off. Because if you believe that it's beneficial, then you may help yourself to relax and perform just that little bit better.

A ritual can be just about anything so long as it has a meaning for you.

Proper scientific research into the power of rituals only started a couple of years ago. But further results are starting to come in and they look good. For example, there's evidence that performing a meaningless ritual can help people to eat less, too. The proof comes from a study led by Allen Ding Tian, a talented researcher who at the time was splitting his time between Shanghai University of Finance and Economics and Wuhan University. The team of scientists recruited several dozen women who were willing to keep diaries listing everything they ate in exchange for gift cards worth just $10 from Starbucks.

Half of the women were told to cut their calories by eating more mindfully. They were instructed every time they ate to pause and think carefully about what they were eating.

The other half of the participants were asked to work through the following ritual:

First, cut your food into pieces before you eat it. Second, rearrange the pieces so that they are perfectly symmetric on your plate. That is,

get the right half of your plate to look exactly the
same as the left half of your plate. Finally, press
your eating utensil against the top of your food
three times.

That's clearly nonsense. But it worked. The participants who
were told to pause and think about their food consumed on
average 1,648 calories a day. The participants who conducted
the pointless ritual ate 1,424 calories a day – that's 13.6% less.[9]

And remember: this was a garbage ritual that the scientists had
made up out of nothing. But it still did the job. So if you were
particularly interested in the health and weight loss techniques
from Chapter 3, you might like to try this one, too.

> There's evidence that performing a meaningless
> ritual can help people to eat less, too

On the other hand, don't force yourself to do a ritual if you
don't want to. The survey by Alison Wood Brooks and her
compatriots found that 46.5% of people used rituals in at least
some high-stakes situations. So that means that quite a lot of
people also do *not* use them. So if you still think that this ritual
business sounds like rubbish and you can't remember a time
when you have ever performed one, then forget it. Try the
other techniques from this chapter instead.

Onwards and upwards

- To boost your performance in public speaking and other anxiety-
  provoking situations, spend a few minutes beforehand writing
  about a related situation in which you once experienced success.
  However, remember to write about a specific situation rather than

similar situations in general; doing so may help you to not only feel better but perform demonstrably better, too.

- Think constantly about your posture. Better posture really seems to pay off: not only does your posture affect how you think and feel about yourself but also it measurably changes how other people perceive you. So if you want to make a strong impression and be remembered for the right reasons, bear in mind that your posture really does matter.

- Even highly skilled and practised performers can choke in the face of pressure. If you think that's likely for you, make a conscious decision to reframe challenging circumstances in a more positive manner. Imagine how a good friend or a supporter might encourage you to see what's happening to you. Or remind yourself that it may feel like a life and death situation – but you won't actually die. Look at the situation in a different way and you may help yourself to reduce the pressure and perform at your more usual level.

- If you believe that performing a ritual may help to boost your luck, then by all means keep on doing so. Remember that a ritual can be any sequence of actions that *you* believe will be helpful to your subsequent performance. So whether you're prepping for a sales meeting or a sporting confrontation, you may genuinely be able to help yourself to perform better.

8

Finding small ways to feel happier

'If you want to be happy, be.'

Leo Tolstoy

What do you want out of life? Ask people and many reply that they simply want to be happy.

Clearly, happiness relies on a huge number of things. Most people think they would be happier if they were earning more – or at least not having to worry about bills and rent or the mortgage. Many people worry about the state of the world: politics, crime, pollution, the economy, terrorism, climate change, unemployment, and global pandemics. I've even been reading recently about how the rise of artificial intelligence may eventually give rise to killer robots.

Yes, there's a lot going on around us that can dent our happiness. But psychology teaches us that we can genuinely increase our level of happiness relatively quickly.

In our eighth and final chapter, then, we will look at five proven methods for boosting your happiness. I'm not saying that you can achieve a state of perfect, blissful contentment. But by using a combination of techniques, you can make a small difference here, a bit more of a difference there – and it may all add up to something quite worthwhile.

> Psychology teaches us that we can genuinely increase our level of happiness relatively quickly.

Choosing to be happy

In March, my partner and I bought a new car, a Renault Captur. And ever since, we keep spotting other Capturs on the road. The thing is, the Captur has been one of Renault's best-selling cars for several years. So there were already tens of thousands of Capturs on the roads before we bought ours – we just hadn't noticed them.

The same thing happened when we brought home our first dog, a Miniature Schnauzer. Before bringing him into our lives, we had only ever noticed one of his breed. But since then, we keep spotting them all over the country and even on TV, too.

That's how human nature works. When something is important to us – when we choose to pay attention to something – we are more likely to spot more of it in the future. And it turns out that the same is more or less true for happiness: when you focus your attention on what's good in your life, you help yourself to feel more positive.

> When you focus your attention on what's good in your life, you help yourself to feel more positive.

Back in Chapter 3, we looked at how practising gratitude not only boosted people's well-being – it also had the added benefit of increasing how much exercise they went on to do. To do the exercise, you would write about the things in your life that you felt grateful about. For example, you may be grateful for the support, guidance, or friendship of certain individuals. You may be thankful for opportunities you have been granted in your work. Or you may be glad about certain personal traits or characteristics that you have. And that gratitude exercise is a good example of how focusing our attention on something positive allows us to notice more positive moments, which ultimately helps us to feel happier, too.

But it turns out that there's an even more powerful method for increasing our levels of happiness: it's called the best possible self (BPS) exercise. This involves spending time imagining how your life might turn out in the future, assuming that everything has turned out well. To do this exercise, you would write down what you would like to achieve not only in your work but also in your personal life – for example in terms of your relationships with friends and loved ones. You would also think about the skills and traits you might wish to develop within yourself, too.

However, this isn't an exercise in pure fantasy. You would need to be realistic and choose a set of goals and desires that you think you could actually achieve.

Studies have shown that both the gratitude exercise and the BPS exercise benefit psychological health. Compared to control writing exercises – for example in which people simply kept a daily diary of the things that happened to them – both of the writing activities have been found to boost people's well-being. One of the first and most famous studies was conducted in the United States by Kennon Sheldon of the University of Missouri-Columbia and Sonja Lyubomirsky of the University of California, Riverside.[1] And the same result was replicated years later by Dutch researchers led by Madelon Peters at Maastricht University in the Netherlands.[2]

However, these and other studies suggest that the BPS exercise may even have a slight advantage over the gratitude exercise.[3] So I'm going to take you through the BPS exercise now. It involves an initial investment of around 20 minutes followed by a few minutes of further thinking every day.

Imagining your best possible self

Several dozen studies by different groups of researchers spread across the globe have investigated the benefits of the best possible self (BPS) exercise. When I introduce this technique to clients, I usually explain that there are three steps involved:

Step 1: To begin with, spend just one minute thinking about your best possible self. Imagine yourself some years in the future and that everything has gone well for you. You have worked hard and accomplished all of the goals that you could realistically have hoped to achieve. How does this future life look?

Step 2: Next, spend around 15 to 20 minutes writing about what is going on in this ideal future life of yours. Think in particular about three areas of your life: your relationships, your work, and your personal characteristics. In terms of your relationships, what would you like to be happening with your friends, loved ones, colleagues, and the other people in your life? In your work, what would you like to achieve in terms of your accomplishments, position, skills, level of expertise, and so on? Finally, what would you like to change and develop with respect to your personal characteristics, your strengths and weaknesses, traits and qualities? Make notes on each of these three areas and then try to combine your notes into a coherent story that incorporates your thoughts and feelings, as if you are writing a summary of what has already happened to you.

Step 3: For the next two weeks, spend five minutes every day visualizing a different area of your best possible future. On different days, think about your relationships or your work or your personal characteristics. As you do this daily visualization, consider not only what your life would look like but also how you would feel if you had achieved this ideal future.

By the way, if the BPS writing exercise looks familiar, that's probably because we encountered something similar in Chapter 1. That exercise for beating the effects of stress and boosting physical health involved a one-off writing exercise.

In contrast, this three-step BPS exercise is one of the longer interventions contained within the pages of this book. It requires around 20 minutes on one day, followed by a further five minutes a day for two weeks. It's not an immediate fix. But trust the very robust science behind it. Studies have shown that deliberately choosing to pay attention to your life goals in a positive way may help to rewire your brain. You could help yourself in just a matter of weeks to develop a more optimistic outlook on life.

> Deliberately choosing to pay attention to your life goals in a positive way may help to rewire your brain.

Improving your life balance

Many people complain about their work–life balance, the degree to which their work, studies, chores, or other obligations impinge upon their family and personal lives. In simple terms, people who feel they have too much to do every day don't feel terribly happy.

As I'm sure you've guessed, I'm leading up to telling you about a technique that you can use to boost your overall satisfaction with life. But let's take things one step at a time. And the first step involves you analysing how you typically spend your time.

Think about an average day. I appreciate that your schedule probably varies from one day to the next. But for the purposes of this exercise, try to think about what a typical or more average day may look like. In the table below, I have set out 10 areas of life – and I'd like you to estimate how much time you spend doing each. This is just a hypothetical exercise, so don't spend huge amounts of time trying to calculate exactly how long you spend doing each. It should only take you a few minutes to write the number of hours you spend on each activity into the appropriate 'time spent' boxes.

For example, you likely sleep somewhere between 4 and 10 hours a day. Perhaps you spend a handful of hours commuting. And if you're like most people, you probably spend a large number of hours at work or studying – or both. There is also an 'other' category at the bottom of the list. If you do any activity that's not on the list, please add it. For instance, if you're a full-time but unpaid caregiver, you would probably want to include that. And if you don't spend any time doing one or more of the activities, then you would simply put a zero in those boxes.

Remember that there are only 24 hours in a day. So your sums have to add up. The hours that you allocate to the 10 activities must total to 24!

Area of your life	Time spent	Time goal
Sleep (time in bed)		
Paid work (time spent at work)		
Study (time spent studying and in class)		
Chores (time spent cooking, cleaning, buying food, etc.)		
Community (time with groups, clubs, etc.)		
Recreation (time on sports, TV, devices, music, etc.)		
Commuting (time spent getting to and from work or study)		
Personal relationships (time with family, friends, partner)		
Health and self-care (time exercising, eating, washing, etc.)		
Spirituality/religion (time meditating or doing religious duties)		
Other:		
Total	24	24

Sorry if I'm repeating myself, but once you've put your numbers into the 'time spent' column, do check that they add up to 24.

The next step is then to think about how you would ide-ally allocate your time. In the 'time goal' column, now think about how you would like to spend your time, if you could. Of course you have certain constraints in your life that you can't change. But what could you change? Could you free up just a little time here and there to make just enough space for you to invest in the things you personally find important? Perhaps you want a little more sleep or time with your family. Maybe you want to read more business books or the freedom to engage in a hobby or something else entirely. As before, though, your total must add up to exactly 24.

The third and final step is to think about actual actions you could take in order to change how you generally spend your time and get closer to your ideal time allocation. So what actions could you take over the next four weeks?

By this stage, you've already figured out what your ideal 24-hour day would involve. It's now a case of figuring out things you could do differently to move closer to this ideal.

You probably won't be able to achieve this ideal schedule exactly. And of course there will be some days when it may be completely impossible. But even small changes in terms of how you spend your time may help you to feel more in control and happier with your life.

> Even small changes in terms of how you spend your time may help you to feel more in control and happier with your life.

As this is the final chapter of the book, I'm sure you have no doubt guessed that this isn't just some exercise that I made up.

The life balance method was created by a team of international collaborators from the US, Australia, and India. More importantly, the researchers Kennon Sheldon from the University of Missouri–Columbia, Robert Cummins from Deakin University, and Shanmukh Kamble from Karnatak University have found that the 'life balance' method works. Over the course of four weeks, experimental participants who successfully altered their time allocations reported higher levels of subjective well-being.[4]

Designing the perfect day

Remember that there are three broad steps to the life balance method. First of all, work out how you tend to spend the average day. Count how many hours you typically spend on commuting, sleep, recreation, and other activities.

Secondly, work out how you would *like* to spend your time. Be positive but also realistic. You probably can't just cut your working hours in half. Neither can you transport yourself instantaneously to your office or place of work.

Thirdly, have a good think about actions you could take to spend your time in the more desirable way. Perhaps, for example, you could say no a little more often or prioritize more carefully and ignore just a few tasks or chores entirely. Maybe you could work from home occasionally. Could you commute either earlier or later in the day before the roads get so busy? Do share your time allocation chart with selected friends or family members and ask for suggestions, too.

Those three steps are all about planning. But perhaps the most challenging part comes in actually putting some of your actions into practice. Messy reality will often get in the way: problems and hassles may conspire to derail your plans. However, perseverance will likely pay off. You may only be able to save a little time here and a little time there. But add up enough small changes and you may well make a measurable difference to your own well-being.

Clearly, the life balance method is not a quick fix. It requires planning, real thought, and perhaps conversations with a friend or two to begin with. And overall, the whole endeavour takes four weeks. But little in life that is worthwhile can be accomplished overnight. The only question now is: are you willing to make the investment to give this evidence-based technique a go?

> Little in life that is worthwhile can be accomplished overnight.

Attuning your awareness to good things

Both the best possible self (BPS) and life balance methods that we have covered so far in this chapter take a handful of weeks to complete. But if you're looking for a near-instantaneous boost to your psychological well-being, you could try a different psychological intervention.

This is called the three good things intervention and it's pretty straightforward. You just need to spend at least five minutes writing about three things that went well for you and why they went well.

And that's all there is to it. Like I said, it's really simple.

Naturally, there's evidence backing up the technique. A team led by the University of Florida's Joyce Bono asked 61 adults to take part in a 15-day experiment. Over the course of the first seven days, the researchers telephoned each of the participants to interview them about their stress levels.

Over the final eight days of the experiment, the participants were instructed at the end of each working day to write down at least three good things that had happened to them that day. For each good thing, the participants were also told to answer the question: 'Why did this good thing happen?' In all, the participants were encouraged to write for between 5 and 10 minutes.

On analysing the results, Bono and her research associates found that the participants who completed the writing exercise before leaving work reported experiencing fewer health complaints during their evenings. The participants also said that they felt more detached from their work and less stressed in general, too.[5]

So notice that the benefits didn't kick in after eight days or even several days. When participants completed the writing exercise before they left work, they felt more invigorated *that same evening*. Like I said then, this is a method that bolsters people rather quickly.

Recording good things

The three good things technique seems to be a way for people to feel both physically and psychologically more invigorated after work. So many of us are almost programmed to grumble about the things that went wrong at work. In contrast, this exercise is a way to train our minds to look deliberately for what is positive in our daily lives. We don't have to spend our evenings fixating unnecessarily on our workday problems or hassles.

To try this exercise, spend five to 10 minutes at the end of your working day writing down:

- Three positive things that happened to you during the day.

- The reason why each thing went well. Answer to your own satisfaction the question: 'Why did this good thing happen?'

It's up to you what you choose to write about. The three good things can be big or small. In reality, few of our days are filled with major achievements or events. Much of the time, simply completing a task successfully, receiving a compliment from a colleague or simply being able to enjoy a walk in the sunshine may be things worth celebrating.

At first, you may find that writing about positive events and the reasons they occur may feel somewhat awkward. Like learning most new skills – playing the violin, speaking a foreign language, riding a skateboard – it can feel unfamiliar or unwieldy. But remember that the three good things exercise is simply a way to reorient your mind so that you can find greater joy in the positive moments that genuinely do come your way each day.

> The three good things exercise is simply a way to reorient your mind so that you can find greater joy in the positive moments that genuinely do come your way each day.

Now, you may have noticed that this exercise bears more than a passing resemblance to the gratitude practice that we examined back in Chapter 3. However, there are a few differences between the two. For example, the three good things exercise is to be done at the end of the working day rather than at the end of the entire day. Also, the three good things exercise asks people to list not only *what* happened but also *why*.

I'm not sure if doing both the gratitude practice from Chapter 3 *and* this three good things exercise will deliver an additive effect. I suspect that doing either one may be beneficial, but that doing both will have an effect that is less than the sum of their parts. Say if one boosts most people's well-being by 10% and the other by 10%, I'm guessing that the combination of the two may only deliver a total uplift of perhaps 12 or 16% – something short of what we might like.

That research hasn't been done. But in my personal opinion, I see many of these techniques as having roughly similar effects: ultimately, the choice of which you choose to implement will depend on your personal preferences. I often think of it as being analogous to choosing a painkiller for a headache. Some people prefer paracetamol; others prefer ibuprofen. Likewise for psychological techniques, there's no right or wrong answer – no remedy that is better or worse for every single person. We all have different tastes and preferences, so choose whichever of the exercises resonates most with you.

> For psychological techniques, there's no right or wrong answer – no remedy that is better or worse for every single person.

Taking more joy from everyday experiences

The Marvel Cinematic Universe is the most successful film franchise in history. The first time I watched *The Avengers* (which was retitled *Avengers Assemble* in the UK), I nearly cried with excitement. I used to read the comics when I was growing up – I started when I was maybe 8 or 9 years old – and I used to love the art, the struggles against supervillains, but also the squabbles amongst the heroes themselves. I was almost fizzing with delight as I watched my childhood heroes up on the big screen. And, as I said, at several moments during the film, I felt so filled with joy that I could feel tears welling up in my eyes.

I've since watched the movie a couple of times but never had the same level of visceral reaction. And that's probably due to a psychological phenomenon called adaptation. The first time we experience something enjoyable, we don't quite know what to expect so our senses are fully engaged. Whether that involves eating a dish we have never tried before, playing a new sport, watching the latest TV show, or anything else, we can't help but be more immersed in it. But the second time becomes just a little less different and special. And so it continues on the third time, the fourth, and so on. The more familiar an experience becomes, the less pleasure we can take from it. In psychological parlance, we have adapted to it.

One implication of psychological adaptation is that we should seek out variety and novelty in our experiences in order to feel positive emotions such as joy more strongly. Simply re-reading the same books, re-watching the same films, eating the same foods over and over again is likely to lead to a more muted appreciation of life.

> We should seek out variety and novelty in our experiences in order to feel positive emotions such as joy more strongly.

Another option is to engage with any experience more mindfully – to focus on it fully and intently as if you were experiencing it for the first time. For example, there are probably dozens of foods that you've eaten time and time again. But imagine that you're from a remote culture and that you have never had a piece of bread, a plate of noodles or pasta, a chocolate bar, or whatever else you're so used to eating. Try to focus on the taste, the texture, the sensations – even the sounds – of every mouthful. People who report eating more mindfully say that they tend to enjoy their foods more. And, incidentally, people who learn to eat more mindfully also tend to eat less and weigh less than people who eat more mindlessly.[6]

But the main point I'm making here isn't about weight loss. It's about engaging with any experience – whether that's a food or a repeat viewing of a favourite film – more mindfully in order to revitalize your enjoyment of it.

There's also a further option, which was discovered in a series of studies by Ed O'Brien at the University of Chicago and Robert Smith at Ohio State University. In one of their studies, the researchers asked participants to eat popcorn – just 10 pieces of it – either with their hands or with a pair of chopsticks. When asked to rate how much they had enjoyed the snack, the participants who ate their popcorn with chopsticks reported having enjoyed it 11.0% more. Eating a familiar food in an unfamiliar fashion had boosted their enjoyment.

In another experiment, the research duo asked participants to rate their enjoyment from watching an exciting video of a motorcycle ride filmed from the driver's perspective. The video was then shown two more times, but with the participants split into two groups on the third showing. The first half of the participants watched the video in a conventional fashion as they had the previous two times. But the other half was instructed to watch using so-called hand goggles – using their thumbs and index fingers to form circles around their eyes and using them to track the ride, for example to bob their heads left or right when the driver turned in one direction or the other.

The participants who watched the video in the usual fashion reported less enjoyment on the second viewing and even less on the third – demonstrating the principle of adaptation. But the participants who watched through their fingers reported finding the video nearly as thrilling as the very first time. Again, the unconventional practice boosted their enjoyment.[7]

Across a sequence of studies involving different types of experiences and media, O'Brien and Smith came to the same conclusion over and over again: in order to recapture how we feel about experiences we've already had, we could benefit from consuming old things in new ways.

In order to recapture how we feel about experiences we've already had, we could benefit from consuming old things in new ways.

Recapturing first-time experiences

It's human nature to derive less enjoyment from experiences we've already had. For this reason, the old English adage that 'variety is the spice of life' may actually be true; consuming new things may help us to experience life more vividly. However, there are two further ways in which to recapture how you feel about experiences you've already had.

- Consume the experience mindfully. In modern life, we're so often in a rush that we may consume certain experiences without fully appreciating them. For example, many of us eat dinner while watching TV. Or we may watch Netflix while also checking Instagram and messaging friends. But studies suggest that concentrating fully and intently on one experience at a time may be a better way to enjoy that experience properly.

- Consume an old experience in a new way. The work by O'Brien and Smith suggests that it's possible to overcome psychological adaptation simply by changing how we consume experiences. The added benefit is that revisiting old experiences may be cheaper, less wasteful, or less time-consuming, too. So use your imagination to see what novel methods you can come up with.

I am reluctant to give you examples of unconventional ways of consuming old experiences. What works for one person may seem bothersome or ridiculous for others. For example, at university I had a friend who briefly discovered that she enjoyed drinking coffee out of a bowl rather than a cup. But that struck me as a silly idea.

I could imagine putting blankets and pillows on the floor and creating a den from which to watch a favourite movie rather than just sitting on the sofa. But perhaps you might think that too uncomfortable or inconvenient. You might decide to move your sofa much closer to your TV and to turn the sound up much louder. Or to sit completely naked while watching the film. Or to invite friends over to watch the film again dressed up as characters from the movie. Or maybe you would rather go to see it again at an outdoor cinema under a starry sky.

There's no one method that will work for everyone. The point is simply this: to revitalize the pleasure you take from past, treasured experiences, see if you can find different ways of engaging with them.

> To revitalize the pleasure you take from past, treasured experiences, see if you can find different ways of engaging with them.

Investing in your relationship

A romantic partner can be a source of great happiness – but also great unhappiness. In most countries in the Western world, somewhere between 40 and 50% of marriages end in divorce. Even when couples choose not to get divorced, that doesn't mean that they are always happy – some couples struggle on together for years despite feeling disgruntled and less than entirely satisfied.

If you're in a relationship, how much time would you invest in being happier together? Is your relationship worth just seven minutes of your time?

Is your relationship worth just seven minutes of your time?

The brief writing exercise I'm about to share with you has been extensively tested by a collective of psychological scientists. Led by Eli Finkel, a professor of psychology at Northwestern University, the team tracked the marital satisfaction of 120 heterosexual married couples for a full year. Half of the couples were merely monitored for a year – they completed questionnaires every four months rating the extent to which they agreed with statements such as, 'I feel satisfied with our relationship' and, 'I am committed to maintaining my relationship with my partner'. The other half of the couples were also asked once every four months to complete the same questionnaires; in addition, these couples were told to spend a mere seven minutes learning how to think differently about their relationship conflicts and disagreements.

In psychological terms, the technique is called emotional reappraisal – it's about learning to see upsetting situations in a less negative fashion. And after a full 12 months, Finkel and his associates found that the couples who had been taught emotional reappraisal reported feeling quantifiably more satisfied with their relationships than the couples who had just been passively monitored.[8]

For me, this study illustrates that having a long, satisfying relationship is not just about finding the one person in the world who is perfect for you. The happy ending doesn't happen automatically. Happy relationships require work on an ongoing basis. In this instance, a relatively modest investment of time in a straightforward mental exercise may allow you to make a meaningful difference to your relationship.

> Happy relationships require work on an ongoing basis.

Writing your way to relationship satisfaction

To boost your relationship satisfaction, you and your partner both need to complete this emotional reappraisal exercise. I suggest that you work through the steps independently: you don't need to do it at the same time or even in the same place as your partner – you never need to show what you've written to each other, either. Finkel and his collaborators found that doing this exercise once every four months was enough to produce a measurable benefit in terms of relationship quality.

- Begin by spending a few minutes writing about the most significant disagreement you had with your partner over the last four months. Avoid writing about your thoughts or feelings. As far as possible, write a fact-based summary of what actually happened.

- Next comes the reappraisal part: think about this disagreement from the perspective of a neutral third party. Imagine that this individual wants the best for you and your partner but has an impartial point of view. What might this unbiased observer think about the disagreement? How might this onlooker find the good that could come about as a result of it?

- Consider that many people find it helpful to take this third-party perspective during disagreements with their romantic partner. Of course, it's not easy to take this neutral, third-party perspective at all times. So now consider: in your relationship, what obstacles get in the way of you taking this third-party perspective when you're having a disagreement with your partner?

- Finally, think about how you can adopt this third-party viewpoint more of the time in the coming four months. Write down any ideas you may have on how you might help yourself to be more successful at adopting this third-party perspective. And finally write down at least one way in which embracing this perspective is likely to benefit you and your relationship.

Many of the interventions in this book are incredibly simple – some of them take mere moments to do. This relationship revitalization exercise has a few more steps and needs doing every four months or so – think of it like a vaccination, a booster to pep up your relationship. But still, 21 minutes a year isn't really that much to ask, is it?

Onwards and upwards

- To boost your sense of optimism, work through the three steps of the best possible self (BPS) exercise. Write about how you hope your life will turn out for the better in terms of your relationships, your professional life, and your personal traits and qualities. And then revisit that positive future picture by visualizing it daily for two weeks.

- Use the life balance method to work out how you usually spend your time. Then figure out how you would *ideally* like to spend your time. This is a method aimed at making a real difference to your life, so give yourself four weeks to make meaningful changes. But making even relatively small shifts in how you schedule things in could make a measurable difference to your happiness and well-being.

- For a quick (but possibly smaller) boost to your happiness each evening, try the three good things exercise. As you end the working day, write about three positive moments as well as why they occurred. Do this and you may help yourself to detach more successfully from your work, drive down your stress levels, and feel more physically invigorated.

- Taking pleasure from our favourite things is one way to experience joy and happiness. But we know that overfamiliarity with the things we enjoy or even love can sometimes lead to boredom. To restore the delight you take from those precious things, consider consuming them in just a slightly different way. Be creative. Use your ingenuity to change the circumstances in which you watch your favourite movie, read a much-loved book, eat a favourite food, or enjoy a cherished pastime. Do that and you may reignite your joy in such things again.

- Consider that your romantic partner – your boyfriend, girlfriend, husband, or wife – can be either a source of great happiness or unhappiness in your life. To boost your relationship satisfaction, use the reappraisal writing exercise to change how you view conflicts in your relationship. If you and your partner can do the four-step exercise just once every four months, you may see a small but measurable change in the quality of your relationship.

Conclusions

Onwards, upwards, and over to you

'Discipline is the bridge between goals and accomplishment.'

Mother Teresa

This book is ultimately about doing things differently (better!) and achieving your goals. And the great thing is that the simple techniques we've covered can be used by just about anyone. You don't have to have any particular skills, background, or education to benefit from them.

You could have multiple degrees and be an award-winning professional. Or you could be the kind of person who hated school. You could be an office worker, a teacher, an airline pilot, a chef, a caregiver, a tennis coach, anything. All you need is the desire to improve your circumstances and the willingness to invest a little time in working through the appropriate techniques and exercises.

> The simple techniques we've covered can be used by just about anyone.

I've seen so many clients achieve real change in their lives. Usually, that takes a period of many months rather than weeks. But I have seen client after client after client improve their lives and achieve their goals.

For instance, a 29-year-old accounts assistant called Gavin came to me because he was about to lose his job. His employer announced that most of his department was going to be shut down. He felt paralysed by worry over the whole job hunting process, but particularly the idea of having to go for job interviews.

Over the course of several sessions – some face-to-face and some via Skype – we worked towards securing him a new job. First of all, I encouraged him to keep his worries in perspective by thinking about his distant future. To assuage his fears, I asked him to envision and write about the future, a technique that we covered in Chapter 1 that has been shown to reduce stress.

Then I encouraged him to use the backward planning technique (from Chapter 2) to figure out all of the things he needed to do: rewrite his CV, look for new opportunities online, get in touch with recruiters, rehearse answers to likely interview answers, send off applications, research employers, and so on.

Later, we worked to hone his confidence and impact. For instance, I told him that he could help himself to stay motivated by using self-talk that was phrased in the third-person (e.g. 'You can do it, Gavin!') rather than the first-person (e.g. 'I can do it!') – a technique that we covered right at the very beginning of this book, in the Introduction. Plus I suggested a series of back-strengthening exercises in order to improve his posture (Chapter 7), which would ultimately help him to feel and appear more confident.

Another example: Bianca, a 50-something office manager who was looking to make a dramatic career change. I began working with her just after she had started on the route to retraining as a nutritional advisor. To help her to study more effectively and get through her exams, I recommended that she overhaul her entire study approach using techniques from Chapter 6. Specifically, I encouraged her to spend much more time on outputting than inputting – on testing herself rather than simply reading through notes or watching and re-watching online videos.

Several months after we started working together, her oldest, teenage son got into severe difficulties at school and was diagnosed with depression and anxiety. Bianca felt quite overwhelmed with her full-time job, her studies, and trying to support her son. On a practical level, we spent time planning her schedule so that she could fit in her work, study, and other activities. But rather than doing this from the first-person perspective, Bianca found it helpful to imagine that she was planning for someone else who also happened to be called Bianca (a technique from Chapter 4). I also taught her the importance of setting goals that involved approaching what she wanted rather than avoiding what she didn't want; we then broke her goals down into a series of specific implementation intentions (both techniques from Chapter 2).

There were plenty of other interventions I introduced her to (many of which I unfortunately couldn't squeeze into this book). But a final technique she did find useful was to spend a few minutes at the end of each day writing about the things for which she felt grateful (from Chapter 3).

I'm not saying that the precise techniques that helped Gavin and Bianca will necessarily be best for you. Perhaps you're struggling to make a decision and could use the sequential tournament method from Chapter 4. If you're looking to lose weight or otherwise improve your health, then the values exercise from Chapter 3 may be a good start. Or if you need to perform well at an audition, competition, or job interview, maybe try writing about past successes or developing a confidence-boosting ritual (both from Chapter 7). The point is only that the techniques within this book can help you to become a better version of yourself – you can beat stress, boost your motivation, lose weight, and achieve more of your goals in life – so long as you *actually use them.*

The techniques within this book can help you to become a better version of yourself so long as you actually use them.

Matching the right techniques to your personal tastes

In the eight chapters of *10% Better*, I have introduced many different techniques. However, I suspect that you will not find every single one useful.

To explain why, let me ask you a question: what's your favourite drink? More specifically, when you have cooked a meal at home or are perhaps dining out at a restaurant, what do you like to drink while you're eating? Maybe you like beer. Some people like wine. Me personally, I like still water. Even if you offered me a glass of champagne, I'd actually prefer a glass of tap water to go with my food because that way I can really focus on the tastes and textures of my food.

When it comes to most experiences in life, there is no one single 'best' option. If I were to tell you my favourite books, films, TV shows, foods, travel destinations, or social experiences, I imagine that you would probably disagree with most of them – you have your own preferences, after all. Our tastes and preferences can be very individual. And psychologists are increasingly discovering that the same is true when it comes to psychological techniques and interventions, too.

Take the gratitude practice, for example. I covered this back in Chapter 3 – it's what I call a win–win–win technique. You may remember that researchers Robert Emmons and Michael McCullough showed that writing about things that people felt grateful for helped them to feel happier and healthier – they ended up doing more physical exercise, too.

A more recent study led by Carolyn Winslow at George Mason University looked specifically at the benefits of a work-based gratitude technique. Emmons and McCullough's participants were encouraged to write about anything in life that they felt grateful about. In contrast, Winslow's participants were asked to record only work-related things for which they felt grateful.

A month later, Winslow's participants reported feeling no better than other participants who had not been taught the gratitude technique. OK. Maybe that's not entirely surprising. After all, we all have bad days at work. Occasionally, we have awful days at work. So perhaps Winslow's work-based gratitude exercise didn't produce any benefits because people may generally find it easier to point out the highlights in their lives outside of work.

However, further analysis by Winslow and her compatriots found that the work-based gratitude exercise did benefit *some* people. Specifically, people who described themselves as more trusting and less likely to find fault with others experienced significant bumps in their psychological well-being.[1]

In other words, some people benefitted from the psychological exercise more than others. This kind of research looking at who gets the benefits from particular techniques is very much in its infancy – there's not a lot of it around yet. But the point is this: I don't expect that every technique within this book will work for you.

Even an intervention that gets great results for one of your closest friends or a colleague at work may leave you cold (or vice versa). You will need to try out the different methods to see which ones you feel delivers the best results for you.

> Even an intervention that gets great results for one of your closest friends or a colleague at work may leave you cold.

You need to be smart about getting better. And to do that, I suggest that you consider yourself both scientist and experimental participant. You as the experimental participant will have to undertake the different techniques and exercises within this book. But after trying out each one, you as the scientist will have to study the results to decide whether it delivered enough of a result. If it did: great. If it didn't, perhaps try again or try something different.

Creating the perfect programme for bettering yourself

Back in Chapter 2, I explained that people tend to be much more successful at achieving their goals when they break their overall goals into a number of more explicit commitments. You may remember that we discussed research on implementation intentions, which take the form of 'If... then...' statements. (You may want to turn back to the section 'Specifying when and how you want to succeed' and in particular the box 'Turning broad goals into specific actions', too.)

So now it's your turn. Whatever your overall goals, try to turn them into a set of more specific commitments that you are making. What will you do – and exactly when will you do it?

For example, suppose you want your colleagues to see you as a more capable and confident person and you think you might like to try out the positive recall technique from Chapter 7. You could write an implementation intention commitment to yourself that says something like: 'If I am getting ready for my weekly team meeting, then I will spend five minutes writing about a specific past, positive experience.'

Or if you're trying to be more creative in life, perhaps you might decide upon commitments such as, 'If I need to do some creative thinking at the start of a project, then I will go to the café next door for an hour' and, 'If I need to do some creative thinking, then I will begin by spending 10 minutes writing about the project as if I am a 7-year-old.'

The precise commitments you make will depend on two things: first of all, what your goals are – to do with fitness, stress, happiness, studying, and so on – and, secondly, the actual psychological techniques you wish to try. It really is up to you to come up with implementation intention statements that will suit your needs. Just trust in the research: take a few minutes to translate your overarching goals into specific implementation intention commitments and you give yourself a much better chance of achieving them.

Setting yourself up for success

How many separate implementation intentions should you aim for? Or, as clients sometimes ask me: what's the maximum number of implementation intentions you should allow yourself?

In my work with clients, I do not say that there is an ideal number that works for everyone. In fact, the best or maximum number of implementation intentions will vary for different people. I think the best way to decide the right number for any one person is to ask: 'How confident in percentage terms do you feel that you can achieve all of the implementation intentions you've set out to do?'

How confident in percentage terms do you feel that you can achieve all of the implementation intentions you've set out to do?

For example, say you identify 17 separate implementation intentions that you could apply to your life in areas such as your performance at work, your relationship with your partner, and your eating and health. Imagine me asking you: 'How confident in percentage terms do you feel that you can achieve all 17 of these implementation intentions?'

It's not a question that you should answer immediately. I encourage you to think about it this way: would you bet, say, the price of a dinner at your favourite restaurant on you achieving all of the implementation intentions you have said you would like to do?

Perhaps you feel only 60% confident that you can achieve everything. In which case, I would argue that you may be taking on too much. I usually encourage clients to pick a number of implementation intentions at which they feel around 80% confident that they can follow through on everything.

So, for some people, that may be a very small number of implementation intentions – just two or three, perhaps. For the fortunate minority who know that they have rock-solid willpower, they may feel confident enough to do not only the 17 implementation intentions but a few more than that, too.

Of course, there's science behind asking you how confident you feel about your goals. Studies by Timur Sevincer at the University of Hamburg and Gabriele Oettingen at New York University have shown that people's expectations of success really do predict – at least somewhat – the results that they will get. People who feel more confident that they will get good results tend to get genuinely better results than people who are more noncommittal.[2]

> People's expectations of success really do predict – at least somewhat – the results that they will get.

But here's the thing: you have to be honest with yourself. Only you know if you're very confident, somewhat confident, or not very confident about the goals – the implementation intentions – you have set yourself.

So before you commit to your list of implementation intentions, take a good look at them. How confident do you really feel about them?

Perhaps you kind of suspect that your list is probably going to be too much. Or maybe you know that a few of the actions on your list aren't terribly likely. For example, you may know that you're good at achieving intellectual goals that you set for yourself, such as wanting to read a certain number of non-fiction books in a year or studying in order to pass an exam. But deep down you may realize that you're less good with physical goals, such as going to the gym or saying no to junk food. Or perhaps it's the other way around – you're not so good with academic goals but good with sports and your health.

Clearly, it's not a good idea to set yourself too much to do – you may just end up feeling disillusioned when you don't achieve it all. It's a better idea to set yourself a smaller list of implementation intentions that you can accomplish in their entirety.

> It's not a good idea to set yourself too much to do – you may just end up feeling disillusioned when you don't achieve it all.

And if you're not feeling entirely confident that you can achieve everything on your list, you can also have a think about practical ways to boost your confidence levels. What everyday tips or methods could you use to turn your implementation intentions into real action? For example, there are lots of apps that you can install on your phone to ping up reminders of actions that you should be taking. Maybe some of them could help you to keep track of your commitments and give you a better shot at success.

Maybe you could write your implementation intentions on pieces of paper and then tape them to your fridge, your bathroom mirror, your car dashboard, or anywhere else you like. Or scribble them on Post-it notes. Perhaps share your commitments with a partner or a couple of friends and give them permission to prompt you about them occasionally. Do whatever you think will help *you* to succeed.

Just remember: put together a list of implementation intentions that you feel at least 80% certain you can complete. When you've achieved everything on your initial list, you can always come back and add more stuff to it later.

> Put together a list of implementation intentions that you feel at least 80% certain you can complete.

Consider that it's better to set yourself too little to do and then achieve it. Seeing yourself accomplishing your goals will fuel your confidence and make you motivated to do even more. Set yourself too much to do and you could trigger the opposite pattern of behaviour: you may end up denting your confidence and reducing your motivation to continue.

Honestly, then, set yourself a super easy target. Just do a few things to begin with and you may soon see your success growing like a snowball rolling down a mountain.

Taking your first steps to being better

OK. We're nearly at the end of the book. If you want to read more of my advice on an ongoing basis, then do track me down on social media. And I get a big kick out of hearing from readers, so do let me know what you thought of *10% Better* – or what else you'd like me to write about!

www.facebook.com/drrobyeung

www.instagram.com/doctorrobyeung

www.twitter.com/robyeung

Over the course of the last couple of hundred pages, we've covered a lot of different topics and techniques. And hopefully, you have an idea of what you want to work on. But don't worry if you're not entirely sure where to begin. I'll leave you with one final exercise that you can use to get started – it involves four steps and will only take you around a minute per step.

The technical name of the exercise is mental contrasting with implementation intentions, but I call it the GOMP method because those four letters describe the four steps. Ultimately, the name isn't important – all that matters is that dozens of experiments have shown that it genuinely helps people to feel more energized in pursuing and realizing their goals.[3]

To make it work for you, you need to begin by thinking about a goal and what it would look like. Then you identify the biggest mental block in your way and finally come up with a one-sentence plan of action. Here are the four steps/questions for you to work through:

1. Goal – in a sentence, what is your goal? Choose one realistic goal that you reckon you can accomplish within a month. So even if you want to change lots of things in your life, start with just one goal for now.

2. Outcome – what would it look and feel like to accomplish your goal? Picture in your head that you have achieved a positive outcome. Take around a minute to immerse yourself in this mental scene of what it would look, sound, and feel like.

3. Mental block – what's the biggest psychological barrier in your way? That could be your mood or a belief, a personality trait or a bad habit. Take a minute here to identify the deep-down mental obstacle that's holding you back from making progress with your goal.

4. Plan – what could you plan to do to overcome the mental block in order to get started? Write this down as an 'If… then…' implementation intention so that when your mental block crops up you are committing to do or say something to yourself to try to overcome that mental block.

For example, say someone called Jeremiah wants to get fitter and lose some weight – he identifies that as his step 1 goal. Next, he would take a few moments to visualize how he would look and how it would feel to him to get fitter: maybe he sees his toned reflection in a mirror or hears in his head the compliments that friends and co-workers might say to him.

Moving on to the third step, perhaps he recognizes that his biggest personal block is hunger – that he often feels so hungry after work that he just wants to eat something rather than exercise. Finally, he comes up with an implementation intention to ensure he eats a snack every afternoon so he isn't so hungry – he writes down: 'If I'm going to exercise that day, then I will buy an apple and a yoghurt at lunchtime and eat them at 4 p.m.'

Or suppose someone called Mirai decides upon a goal that she wants to feel less insecure about her relationship with her boyfriend. She would spend maybe a minute envisioning herself being happy and supportive with her boyfriend. Then she would try to figure out the major psychological issue that stops her from feeling secure – maybe it's that she engages in self-talk that 'He doesn't say enough that he loves me, so he probably doesn't really love me.' To try to overcome that negative self-talk, she decides on the implementation intention: 'If I start to doubt my relationship, then I will boost my mood by looking back at old photos on my phone showing how happy we can be.'

But those are just examples. Your GOMP could look somewhat similar or wildly different. The technique requires that you identify a goal that *you* personally find meaningful. You have to visualize what it would look and feel like for *you*. You have to rummage around in your head to identify the biggest mental obstacle that stops *you* from making progress – it could be something incredibly specific that doesn't bother most other people. And finally you will have to come up with an implementation plan that makes sense to *you* and you alone.

Anyway, the GOMP technique is just one final idea for something that you could try. If you don't like it, try one of the many other exercises or tactics. This book is packed with plenty of proven methods for beating stress, improving your motivation, losing weight, boosting your creativity, improving your relationships, and achieving just about any goal. But in order to become that better version of yourself, you have to use the techniques – not just understand them. So be smart. Do something. Get started.

> In order to become that better version of yourself, you have to use the techniques – not just understand them.

Onwards and upwards

- Consider that the techniques within *10% Better* can help you to beat stress, lose weight, boost your learning, and so on – but only if you actually put them into practice. Merely understanding the techniques won't make that much of a difference. So make a plan as soon as possible to integrate them into your day-to-day life.

- Use the proven 'If… then…' implementation intention format to create your plan of action. Spend just a few moments choosing the right time of day, location, or situation (the 'If…' part) in which you will use any given technique (the 'then…' part).

- Make it easy for yourself to achieve everything in your plan. Aim to have just a small number of implementation intentions that you can confidently complete – this will boost your confidence and allow you to make more changes later on.

- Also bear in mind that you will probably enjoy or benefit more from certain techniques than others. You are an individual with your own particular personality, tastes, and preferences. So accept that you will need a period of trial and error to figure out the mental tricks and methods that work best for you.

- Don't forget to follow Dr Rob on Twitter (@robyeung), Facebook (drrobyeung), or Instagram (@doctorrobyeung) if you want to continue learning, growing, and making yourself better.

- And if you're still stuck on where to start, do consider the GOMP (goal, outcome, mental block, and plan) method for tackling just one small goal. It takes most people less than five minutes to work through it.

Notes

INTRODUCTION

[1] Kross, E., Bruehlman-Senecal, E., Park, J., Burson, A., Dougherty, A., Shablack, H., Bremner, R., Moser, J., & Ayduk, O. (2014). Self-talk as a regulatory mechanism: How you do it matters. *Journal of Personality and Social Psychology, 106,* 304–24.

CHAPTER 1: GETTING SMART ABOUT STRESS AND EVERYDAY PRESSURES

[1] Cohen, S., Kamarck, T., & Mermelstein, R. (1983). A global measure of perceived stress. *Journal of Health and Social Behavior, 24,* 385–96.

[2] Levenstein, S., Prantera, C., Varvo, V., Scribano, M. L., Berto, E., Luzi, C., & Andreoli, A. (1993). Development of the perceived stress questionnaire: A new tool for psychosomatic research. *Journal of Psychosomatic Research, 37,* 19–32.

[3] Markowitsch, H. J., Vandekerckhove, M. M. P., Lanfermann, H., & Russ, M. O. (2003). Engagement of lateral and medial prefrontal areas in the ecphory of sad and happy autobiographical memories. *Cortex, 39,* 643–65.

[4] Speer, M. E., & Delgado, M. R. (2017). Reminiscing about positive memories buffers acute stress responses. *Nature Human Behavior, 1,* Article 0093.

[5] Speer, M. E., Bhanji, J. P., & Delgado, M. R. (2014). Savoring the past: Positive memories evoke value representations in the striatum. *Neuron, 84,* 847–56.

[6] Hystad, S. W., Eid, J., Johnsen, B. H., Laberg, J. C., & Bartone, P. T. (2010). Psychometric properties of the revised Norwegian dispositional resilience (hardiness) scale. *Scandinavian Journal of Psychology, 51*, 237–45.

[7] Hystad, S. W., Eid, J., & Brevik, J. I. (2011). Effects of psychological hardiness, job demands, and job control on sickness absence: A prospective study. *Journal of Occupational Health Psychology, 16*, 265–78.

[8] Teisman, T., Het, S., Grillenberger, M., Willutzki, U., & Wolf, O. T. (2013). Writing about life goals: Effects on rumination, mood and the cortisol awakening response. *Journal of Health Psychology, 19*, 1410–19.

[9] Harrist, S., Carlozzi, B. L., McGovern, A. R., & Harrist, A. W. (2007). Benefits of expressive writing and expressive talking about life goals. *Journal of Research in Personality, 41*, 923–30.

[10] Nabi, H., Kivimäki, M., Batty, G. D., Shipley, M. J., Britton, A., Brunner, E. J., Vahtera, J., ... & Singh-Manous, A. (2013). Increased risk of coronary heart disease among individuals reporting adverse impact of stress on their health: The Whitehall II prospective cohort study. *European Heart Journal, 34*, 2697–705.

[11] Kushlev, K., & Dunn, E. W. (2015). Checking email less frequently reduces stress. *Computers in Human Behavior, 43*, 220–8.

[12] Kennedy-Moore, E., & Watson, J. C. (2001). How and when does emotional expression help? *Review of General Psychology, 5*, 187–212.

[13] Wolf, E. B., Lee, J. J., Sah, S., & Brooks, A. W. (2016). Managing perceptions of distress at work: Reframing emotion as passion. *Organizational Behavior and Human Decision Processes, 137*, 1–12.

[14] Galinsky, A. D., Wang, C. S., Whitson, J. A., Anicich, E. M., Hugenberg, H., & Bodenhausen, G. V. (2013). The

reappropriation of stigmatizing labels: The reciprocal relationship between power and self-labeling. *Psychological Science, 24,* 2020–9.

CHAPTER 2: BOOSTING YOUR MOTIVATION AND ACHIEVING YOUR GOALS

[1] Elliot, A. J., Shell, M. M., Henry, K. B., & Maier, M. A. (2005). Achievement goals, performance contingencies, and performance attainment: An experimental test. *Journal of Educational Psychology, 97,* 630–40.

[2] David, M. E., & Haws, K. L. (2016). Saying 'no' to cake or 'yes' to kale: Approach and avoidance strategies in pursuit of health goals. *Psychology & Marketing, 33,* 588–94.

[3] Patrick, V. M., & Hagtvedt, H. (2012). 'I don't' versus 'I can't': When empowered refusal motivates goal-directed behavior. *Journal of Consumer Research, 39,* 371–81.

[4] Dickson, J. M., & Moberly, N. J. (2013). Reduced specificity of personal goals and explanations for goal attainment in major depression. *PLoS ONE, 8,* e64512.

[5] Armitage, C. J. (2007). Effects of an implementation intention-based intervention on fruit consumption. *Psychology & Health, 22,* 917–28.

[6] Wiese, J., Buehler, R., & Griffin, D. (2016). Backward planning: Effects of planning direction on predictions of task completion time. *Judgment and Decision Making, 11,* 147–67.

[7] Park, J., Lu, F.-C., & Hedgcock, W. M. (2017). Relative effects of forward and backward planning on goal pursuit. *Psychological Science, 28,* 1620–30.

[8] Conlon, K. E., Ehrlinger, J., Eibach, R. P., Crescioni, A. W., Alquist, J. L., Gerend, M. A., & Dutton, G. R. (2011). Eyes on the prize: The longitudinal benefits of goal focus on progress toward a weight loss goal. *Journal of Experimental Social Psychology, 47,* 853–5.

CHAPTER 3: BEING SMART ABOUT HEALTH AND WEIGHT LOSS

[1] Falk, E. B., O'Donnell, M. B., Cascio, C. N., Tinney, F., Kang, Y., Lieberman, M. D., … & Strecher, V. J. (2015). Self-affirmation alters the brain's responses to health messages and subsequent behavior change. *PNAS*, *112*, 1977–82.

[2] Brouwer, A. M., & Mosack, K. E. (2015). Motivating healthy diet behaviors: The self-as-doer identity. *Self and Identity*, *14*, 638–53.

[3] Houser-Marko, L., & Sheldon, K. M. (2006). Motivating behavioral persistence: The self-as-doer construct. *Personality and Social Psychology Bulletin*, *32*, 1037–49.

[4] Morewedge, C. K., Huh, Y. E., & Vosgerau, J. (2010). Thought for food: Imagined consumption reduces actual consumption. *Science*, *330*, 1530–3.

[5] Bellieni, C. V., Cordelli, D. M., Raffaelli, M., Ricci, B., Morgese, G., & Buonocore, G. (2006). Analgesic effect of watching TV during venipuncture. *Archives of Disease in Childhood*, *91*, 1015–17.

[6] Braude, L., & Stevenson, R. J. (2014). Watching television while eating increases energy intake: Examining the mechanisms in female participants. *Appetite*, *76*, 9–16.

[7] Mittal, D., Stevenson, R. J., Oaten, M. J., & Miller, L. A. (2010). Snacking while watching TV impairs food recall and promotes food intake on a later TV free test meal. *Applied Cognitive Psychology*, *25*, 871–7.

[8] Stroebele, N., & de Castro, J. M. (2006). Listening to music while eating is related to increases in people's food intake and meal duration. *Appetite*, *47*, 285–9.

[9] Elder, R. S., & Mohr, G. S. (2016). The crunch effect: Food sound salience as a consumption monitoring cue. *Food Quality and Preference*, *51*, 39–46.

[10] Hill, P. L., Allemand, M., & Roberts, B. W. (2013). Examining the pathways between gratitude and self-reported physical health across adulthood. *Personality and Individual Differences*, *54*, 92–6.

[11] Emmons, R. A., & McCullough, M. E. (2003). Counting blessings versus burdens: An experimental investigation of gratitude and subjective well-being in daily life. *Journal of Personality and Social Psychology*, *84*, 377–89.

[12] Kini, P., Wong, J., McInnis, S., Gabana, N., & Brown, J. W. (2016). The effects of gratitude expression on neural activity. *NeuroImage*, *128*, 1–10.

CHAPTER 4: MAKING BETTER DECISIONS

[1] nature has many patterns; employees must be methodical; work in systematic ways; clocks measure time precisely; Jennifer organized her shelves; two-handed typing is efficient; form an orderly queue; investors must be analytical; sunrise times are predictable; solving crimes requires logic.

[2] Rahinel, R., Amaral, N. B., Clarkson, J. J., & Kay, A. C. (2016). On incidental catalysts of elaboration: Reminders of environmental structure promote effortful thought. *Journal of Experimental Social Psychology*, *64*, 1–7.

[3] Schwartz, B., Ward, A., Monterosso, J., Lyubomirsky, S., White, K., & Lehman, D. R. (2002). Maximizing versus satisficing: Happiness is a matter of choice. *Journal of Personality and Social Psychology*, *83*, 1178–97.

[4] Iyengar, S. S., & Lepper, M. R. (2000). When choice is demotivating: Can one desire too much of a good thing? *Journal of Personality and Social Psychology*, *79*, 995–1006.

[5] Iyengar, S. S., Wells, R. E., & Schwartz, B. (2006). Doing better but feeling worse: Looking for the 'best' job undermines satisfaction. *Psychological Science*, *17*, 143–50.

[6] Besedes, T., Deck, C., Sarangi, S., & Shor, M. (2015). Reducing choice overload without reducing choices. *Review of Economics and Statistics*, *97*, 793–802.

[7] Grossman, I., & Kross, E. (2014). Exploring Solomon's Paradox: Self-distancing eliminates the self-other asymmetry in wise reasoning about close relationships in younger and older adults. *Psychological Science*, *25*, 1571–80.

[8] White, R. E., & Carlson, S. M. (2016). What would Batman do? Self-distancing improves executive function in young children. *Developmental Science*, *19*, 419–26.

[9] Polman, E., & Emich, K. J. (2011). Decisions for others are more creative than decisions for the self. *Personality and Social Psychology Bulletin*, *37*, 492–501.

[10] Grossman, I., Sahdra, B. K., & Ciarrochi, J. (2016). A heart and a mind: Self-distancing facilitates the association between heart rate variability, and wise reasoning. *Frontiers in Behavioral Neuroscience*, *10*, Article 68.

CHAPTER 5: BOOSTING YOUR CREATIVITY AND INVENTIVENESS

[1] Zitek, E. M., & Vincent, L. C. (2015). Deserve and diverge: Feeling entitled makes people more creative. *Journal of Experimental Social Psychology*, *56*, 242–8.

[2] Rosenblatt, E., & Winner, E. (1988). The art of children's drawing. *Journal of Aesthetic Education*, *22*, 3–15.

[3] Zabelina, D. L., & Robinson, M. D. (2010). Child's play: Facilitating the originality of creative output by a priming manipulation. *Psychology of Aesthetics, Creativity, and the Arts*, *4*, 57–65.

[4] Skate, water, cream (ice); wheel, high, rocking (chair); out, dog, home (house); lock, line, end (dead); female, flower, friend (girl).

[5] Mehta, R., Zhu, R. (J.), & Cheema, A. (2012). Is noise always bad? Exploring the effects of ambient noise on creative cognition. *Journal of Consumer Research, 39,* 784–99.

[6] Threadgold, E., Marsh, J. E., McLatchie, N., & Ball, L. J. (2019). Background music stints creativity: Evidence from compound remote associate tasks. *Applied Cognitive Psychology, 33,* 873–88.

[7] Oppezzo, M., & Schwartz, D. L. (2014). Give your ideas some legs: The positive effects of walking on creative thinking. *Journal of Experimental Psychology: Learning, Memory, and Cognition, 40,* 1142–52.

[8] Yeung, R. R., & Hemsley, D. R. (1996). Effects of personality and acute exercise on mood states. *Personality and Individual Differences, 20,* 545–50.

[9] Ekkekakis, P., Hall, E. E., VanLanduyt, L. M., & Petruzzello, S. J. (2000). Walking in (affective) circles: Can short walks enhance affect? *Journal of Behavioral Medicine, 23,* 245–75.

[10] Rietzschel, E. F., Nijstad, B. A., & Stroebe, W. (2014). Effects of problem scope and creativity instructions on idea generation and selection. *Creativity Research Journal, 26,* 185–91.

CHAPTER 6: BEING CLEVER ABOUT LEARNING, MEMORY, AND PERFORMANCE

[1] Obesity statistics published on 20 March 2018 by the British government indicated that 61% of adults were either overweight (35%) or obese (a further 26%). For more detailed information, see: Baker, C. (2018). Obesity statistics, *Commons Briefing Papers SN03336.* Retrieved 31 May 2018 from https://researchbriefings. parliament.uk/ResearchBriefing/Summary/SN03336.

[2] I want to emphasize that I am not criticizing the scientists for their research. They were quite clear that their study had been conducted in roundworms. My disapproval is aimed at writers who perhaps chase page clicks by writing sexier headlines

than are warranted by the science. If you are interested in the roundworm research, see: Vohra, M., Lemieux, G. A., Lin, L., & Ashrafi, K. (2017). The beneficial effects of dietary restriction on learning are distinct from its effects on longevity and mediated by depletion of a neuroinhibitory metabolite. *PLoS Biology, 15*, e2002032.

[3] Karpicke, J. D., & Blunt, J. R. (2011). Retrieval practice produces more learning than elaborative studying with concept mapping. *Science, 331*, 772–5.

[4] Forrin, N. D., & MacLeod, C. M. (2018). This time it's personal: The memory benefit of hearing oneself. *Memory, 26*, 574–9.

[5] Goode, S., & Magill, R. (1986). Contextual interference effects in learning three badminton serves. *Research Quarterly for Exercise and Sport, 57*, 308–14.

[6] Carter, C. E., & Grahn, J. A. (2016). Optimizing music learning: Exploring how blocked and interleaved practice schedules affect advanced performance. *Frontiers in Psychology, 7*, Article 1251.

[7] Rohrer, D., Dedrick, R. F., & Burgess, K. (2014). The benefit of interleaved mathematics practice is not limited to superficially similar kinds of problems. *Psychonomic Bulletin Review, 21*, 1323–30.

[8] Monteiro, S., Melvin, L., Manolakos, J., Patel, A., & Norman, G. (2017). Evaluating the effect of instruction and practice schedule on the acquisition of ECG interpretation skills. *Perspectives on Medical Education, 6*, 237–45.

[9] Carvalho, P. F., Braithwaite, D. W., de Leeuw, J. R., Motz, B. A., & Goldstone, R. L. (2016). An *in vivo* study of self-regulated study sequencing in introductory psychology courses. *PLoS ONE, 11*, e0152115.

[10] Propper, R. E., McGraw, S. E., Brunyé, T. T., & Weiss, M. (2013). Getting a grip on memory: Unilateral hand clenching alters episodic recall. *PLoS ONE, 8*, e62474.

CHAPTER 7: DEALING WITH PRESSURE AND PERFORMING IN PUBLIC

[1] Stein, M. B., Walker, J. R., & Forde, D. R. (1996). Public-speaking fears in a community sample: Prevalence, impact on functioning, and diagnostic classification. *Archives of General Psychiatry, 53*, 169–4.

[2] Pezdek, K., & Salim, R. (2011). Physiological, psychological and behavioral consequences of activating autobiographical memories. *Journal of Experimental Social Psychology, 47*, 1214–18.

[3] Nair, S., Sagar, M., Sollers III, J., Consedine, N., & Broadbent, E. (2015). Do slumped and upright postures affect stress responses? A randomized trial. *Health Psychology, 34*, 632–41.

[4] Peper, E., Harvey, R., Mason, L., & Lin, I. M. (2018). Do better in math: How your body posture may change stereotype threat response. *NeuroRegulation, 5*, 67–74.

[5] Veenstra, L., Schneider, I. K., & Koole, S. L. (2016). Embodied mood regulation: The impact of body posture on mood recovery, negative thoughts, and mood-congruent recall. *Cognition and Emotion, 31*, 1361–76.

[6] Balk, Y. A., Adriaanse, M. A., de Ridder, D. T. D., & Evers, C. (2013). Coping under pressure: Employing emotion regulation strategies to enhance performance under pressure. *Journal of Sport & Exercise Psychology, 35*, 408–18.

[7] Nadal, R. (2011). My pre-game rituals sharpen my senses before I go into battle. Retrieved 26 July 2018 from https://www.telegraph.co.uk/sport/tennis/8703175/Rafael-Nadal-my-pre-game-rituals-sharpen-my-senses-before-I-go-into-battle.html.

[8] Brooks, A. W., Schroeder, J., Risen, J. L., Gino, F., Galinsky, A. D., Norton, M. I., & Schweitzer, M. E. (2016). Don't stop believing: Rituals improve performance by decreasing anxiety. *Organizational Behavior and Human Decision Processes, 137*, 71–85.

[9] Tian, A. D., Schroeder, J., Häubl, G., Risen, J. L., Norton, M. I., & Gino, F. (2018). Enacting rituals to improve self-control. *Journal of Personality and Social Psychology, 114*, 851–76.

CHAPTER 8: FINDING SMALL WAYS TO FEEL HAPPIER

[1] Sheldon, K. M., & Lyubomirsky, S. (2006). How to increase and sustain positive emotion: The effects of expressing gratitude and visualizing best possible selves. *Journal of Positive Psychology, 1*, 73–82.

[2] Peters, M. L., Meevissen, Y. M. C., & Hanssen, M. M. (2013). Specificity of the Best Possible Self intervention for increasing optimism: Comparison with a gratitude intervention. *Terapia Psicológica, 31*, 93–100.

[3] For an in-depth look at the merits of the BPS method, see: Malouff, J. M., & Schutte, N. S. (2017). Can psychological interventions increase optimism? A meta-analysis. *Journal of Positive Psychology, 12*, 594–604.

[4] Sheldon, K. M., Cummins, R., & Kamble, S. (2010). Life balance and well-being: Testing a novel conceptual and measurement approach. *Journal of Personality, 78*, 1093–134.

[5] Bono, J. E., Glomb, T. M., Shen, W., Kim, E., & Koch, A. J. (2013). Building positive resources: Effects of positive events and positive reflection on work stress and health. *Academy of Management Journal, 56*, 1601–27.

[6] For an overview of the topic of mindfulness and eating, see: O'Reilly, G. A., Cook, L., Spruijt-Metz, D., & Black, D. S. (2014). Mindfulness-based interventions for obesity-related eating behaviors: A literature review. *Obesity Review, 15*, 453–61.

[7] O'Brien, E., & Smith, R. W. (2019). Unconventional consumption methods and enjoying things consumed: Recapturing the 'first-time' experience. *Personality and Social Psychology Bulletin, 45*, 67–80.

[8] Finkel, E. J., Slotter, E. B., Luchies, L. B., Walton, G. M., & Gross, J. J. (2013). A brief intervention to promote conflict reappraisal preserves marital quality over time. *Psychological Science, 24,* 1595–601.

CONCLUSIONS: ONWARDS, UPWARDS, AND OVER TO YOU

[1] Winslow, C. J., Kaplan, S. A., Bradley-Geist, J. C., Lindsey, A. P., Ahmad, A. S., & Hargrove, A. K. (2017). An examination of two positive organizational interventions: For whom do these interventions work? *Journal of Occupational Health Psychology, 22,* 129–37.

[2] Sevincer, A. T., & Oettingen, G. (2013). Spontaneous mental contrasting and selective goal pursuit. *Personality and Social Psychology Bulletin, 39,* 1240–54.

[3] Oettingen, G., & Reininger, K. M. (2016). The power of prospection: Mental contrasting and behaviour change. *Social and Personality Psychology Compass, 10,* 591–604.

Index